Revolution and Resistance

Suzanne –
thanks for asking
the question
David

Revolution and Resistance

Moral Revolution, Military Might,
and the End of Empire

David Tucker

THE ASHBROOK CENTER
ASHLAND UNIVERSITY

JOHNS HOPKINS UNIVERSITY PRESS   BALTIMORE

© 2016 Johns Hopkins University Press
All rights reserved. Published 2016
Printed in the United States of America on acid-free paper
9 8 7 6 5 4 3 2 1

Johns Hopkins University Press
2715 North Charles Street
Baltimore, Maryland 21218-4363
www.press.jhu.edu

Library of Congress Cataloging-in-Publication Data

Names: Tucker, David, 1951– author.
Title: Revolution and resistance : moral revolution, military might, and the
    end of empire / David Tucker.
Description: Baltimore : Johns Hopkins University Press, [2016] | Includes
    bibliographical references and index.
Identifiers: LCCN 2015049919 | ISBN 9781421420691 (pbk. : alk. paper) | ISBN
    9781421420707 (electronic) | ISBN 1421420694 (pbk. : alk. paper) | ISBN
    1421420708 (electronic)
Subjects: LCSH: Imperialism—History. | United States—Territorial
    expansion—History. | Europe—Territorial expansion—History. |
    Colonies—History. | Anti-imperialist movements—History—20th century. |
    Insurgency—History—20th century. | Irregular warfare—History—20th
    century. | Counterinsurgency—History—20th century. | Military history,
    Modern—20th century.
Classification: LCC E183.7 .T845 2016 | DDC 325/.320973—dc23
    LC record available at https://lccn.loc.gov/2015049919

A catalog record for this book is available from the British Library.

*Special discounts are available for bulk purchases of this book. For more information,
please contact Special Sales at 410-516-6936 or specialsales@press.jhu.edu.*

Johns Hopkins University Press uses environmentally friendly book materials,
including recycled text paper that is composed of at least 30 percent post-consumer
waste, whenever possible.

His Holiness the Pope, by virtue of being Christ's Vicegerent upon earth, piously assumed to himself a right to dispose of the territories of infidels as he thought fit. And in process of time all Christian princes learned to imitate his example, very liberally giving and granting away the dominions and property of Pagan countries. They did not seem to be satisfied with the title which Christianity gave them to the next world only, but chose to infer from thence an exclusive right to this world also.

—Alexander Hamilton, *The Farmer Refuted*

The tie which binds us to our country is not more holy in the sight of God, but it is more deeply seated in our nature, more tender and endearing, than that common link which merely connects us with our fellow-mortal, man.

—John Quincy Adams, *An Address . . . , July 4, 1821*

Contents

Acknowledgments

This book originated in a conversation with Suzanne K. Flinch-baugh, then an editor at Johns Hopkins University Press. She asked if it would be possible to write a brief explanation of the current significance and character of irregular warfare. Grants from the Earhart Foundation allowed me to start and then finish this attempt to answer Suzanne's question. Earlier, a grant from the Smith Richardson Foundation had supported research on French, British, and American counterinsurgency efforts, some of which now appears in altered form in chapter four. Christopher J. Lamb and Patrick Garrity read a draft and offered valuable advice. Chris and I taught a course in the Master's in American History and Government program sponsored by the Ashbrook Center at Ashland University that prompted me to respond affirmatively when Suzanne later asked her question, despite Chris's well-informed skepticism about my arguments. Ellen Tucker read a draft as well and suggested changes. I have benefited in many ways from Ellen's deep knowledge of the Bible and Protestant theology. Comments from anonymous readers for Johns Hopkins University Press were helpful in revising the draft for publication. I am grateful for this support and assistance, and for the efforts of Elizabeth Demers and the staff at Johns Hopkins, as well as Glenn Perkins for his careful editing. A reader who judges this book an unsuccessful response to the question that prompted it will know the author alone is responsible.

Revolution and Resistance

Introduction

Modern history began when Europeans sailed out into the great world to conquer it. That history has been coming to an end for decades now. We live in its prosperous, violent aftermath. Contemporary history is the story of retreat from empire. What will appear in the future, in a world not dominated by European or Euro-American power, we cannot know. It may be that European ideas—democracy, human rights, self-determination—will continue to dominate, at least in speech if not in deed. But they may not. The decline in Euro-American economic and military power, at least relatively, may create the space for alternative accounts to triumph, allowing the sun to set on spiritual as well as physical empire.

With such thoughts in mind, this book provides an account of the rise and decline of Euro-American empire. It argues that events from the Spanish conquest of Mexico to the recent wars in Afghanistan and Iraq are of the same cloth, woven from a set of fundamental ideas and circumstances. These ideas and circumstances shaped not only the conquest of Mexico and the fighting in Iraq but also the way the French dealt with tribes in North America in the eighteenth century and the British controlled India until the twentieth. It argues that a predominant kind of contemporary warfare, irregular warfare—insurgency, terrorism, guerrilla warfare—is best understood in the context of the rise and decline of Euro-American empire over the last 500 years.

The claim made here is not that all irregular warfare over the past 500 years is part of the drama of European global history. Humans have found clever ways to be brutal to one another throughout their history; irregular warfare is coeval with humanity. The focus of the book is on the irregular warfare that occurred as a result of the expansion of Euro-American power and the resistance of those touched by that power. The final two chapters focus on irregular warfare in the twentieth century. They attempt to place that warfare in its proper historical context, to show its true historical significance.

This short book has a long title. A brief review of its contents may help justify it. The first chapter explains how the Europeans conquered much of the world, the moral revolution that encouraged them to do so, the difficulties they faced, and why they did not conquer all of it. Chapter two explains the revolution in warfare and state power that made the conquest possible and the moral revolution that eventually undermined it. Chapter three asks why it was difficult for indigenous people and states to resist European power and how they eventually learned to do it by exploiting certain Euro-American weaknesses: above all, a weakness created by a second moral revolution that began to take hold in Britain and the United States in the late eighteenth century. Chapter four describes how the Europeans, in particular the French, and the Americans tried to overcome indigenous resistance, especially after World War II. The conclusion offers a brief account of some aspects of the current anti-imperial struggle, based on the connections, described in the preceding chapters, between Euro-American imperialism, modernization, and globalization.

While technology, disease, and commerce all help explain the conquest, attitudes and ideas were important as well. Moral revolutions, in particular, were critical for both beginning and ending Euro-American empire and for making irregular warfare—particularly insurgency—an effective means of resistance. In emphasizing the role of morality, especially the moral differences that developed between Europe and the rest of the world, the argument here contends with those (such as Jared Diamond, Daniel R. Headrick, and Ian Morris) who argue that morality, or more accurately, a certain approach to the world, was not responsible for the European conquest. These authors and others object to a claim of European moral superiority. Moral difference is the point stressed in this account. To ignore this difference is to ignore a fundamental aspect of what created, and then undermined, the Euro-American empires.

As well as morality, the military revolution was decisive in building empire. The transition to gunpowder warfare, in association with economic, political, and social changes, led to the creation of a fiscal-military state.

These developments, supported by the first European moral revolution, allowed European states to extract power from their resources more efficiently
than other states or societies and ultimately to project that power overseas.
This gave the Europeans the means of conquest. But behind all these different aspects of the story of the rise and decline of Euro-American empire
lies the distinctive Euro-American freeing of human initiative. This moral
revolution drove expansion, the development of technology, the widening
reach of commerce, and the changing character of the fiscal-military state. It
was a great engine of change; eventually, it even changed itself. This second
moral revolution (the humanitarian revolution) altered the possibilities of
Euro-American empire.

The term "Euro-American empire" needs explanation, both the adjective and the substantive that constitute it. The adjective "Euro-American"
indicates that one of Europe's former colonies rose to preeminence and over
the last years of European dominance was indeed the dominant "European"
power. In the twentieth century, the United States assumed the role of economic and political arbiter that Great Britain played in the nineteenth. In
what follows, it is sometimes possible to distinguish between European and
American approaches to exerting power in the world, just as it is possible to
distinguish the approaches of individual European nations. Where possible,
I make those distinctions.

As the United States assumed the role of political and economic arbiter,
it did so in large part with the purpose of dismantling the European empires.
This was a delayed fulfillment of the American Revolution's anti-imperial
intent. Given that the United States did oppose and undermine European
empires, why is it appropriate to combine the United States with Europe in
the term "Euro-American empire"? The term is used for two reasons. First,
"empire" means the effective exercise of power over space through time. The
test of effective power is to make things happen in that space and during
that time that would not otherwise happen. In this sense, the United States
acts as an empire, extending its power beyond its own borders. Second, the
term "empire" has come to imply the imposition of the imperialists' way of
life on other people. In this sense the term applies to the United States as
well. Americans have frequently believed that they could lead or push the
world into becoming something very much like the United States. This was
an explicit assumption after World War II. A few decades of experience at
the effort tempered expectations and subdued explicit talk of such hopes

but did not destroy the belief. The George W. Bush administration, for example, eventually decided that it had to pay the price and bear the burden of nation building. The purpose was not just to transform the Middle East but to improve the world, to remake it in something like the image of the United States: politically democratic, economically liberal. This transformation would of course benefit the United States, but it would benefit others as well. The altruistic component of American imperialism does not distinguish the United States from European imperialists. The Spanish, Portuguese, French, and British had altruistic motives, first conversion to Christianity and then, especially for the British, conversion to democracy.

For those still not willing to accept the phrase "American empire," and for those all too willing to accept it, the argument that follows offers the reminder that neither Europeans nor Americans invented empire. Empire is almost as old as irregular warfare. Those who take up a practice as universal as it is morally questionable may be given some benefit of the doubt. Also, we now have before us aspirants to imperial sway whose brutality and disregard for freedom can only improve the regard we have for European and American power.

1

Conquest

In 1400, Europe was a remote corner of the Eurasian landmass, marginal to the complex, robust trade system that operated across the Central Asian steppes and the Indian Ocean. China was the world's great power. Gunpowder was invented in China 500 years before it reached Europe. In the tenth and eleventh centuries, China was producing iron and steel in quantities that Europe would not manage for another 600 years. By 1800, China's population was greater than North America's would be in 2014. But Europe was inferior not only to China. For centuries, slaves were Europe's major export to the Islamic world, the center of the Eurasian trade system, a clear sign of the subordinate position of Europe. (As late as the years between 1530 and 1640, Islamic raiders captured and "enslaved around a million western Christian Europeans" [MacCulloch, 57]). So common was such trafficking that the English word "slave" derives from "Slav." Europe was the periphery, sending resources to the Muslim world in exchange for advanced manufactures (Findlay and O'Rourke, 65, 88).

A major unwanted import to Europe from the Eurasian heartland was disease. Originating in Asia, the plague devastated Europe in the middle years of the fourteenth century, killed perhaps half of Europe's population, and recurred periodically and less lethally after that for several centuries. Plague struck London several times in the seventeenth century, in 1665 killing perhaps 20 percent of the city's population.

Well before this, from the time of the Roman empire and even before, various nomadic or tribal peoples from Eurasia—Huns, Mongols, Turks—invaded Europe, plundering and enslaving as they went. Some settled and mixed with the local population, to become the victims of the next wave of invaders. Even in 1600, a hundred years after the European conquests began, Europe was still poor and under threat. The income of the Mughal ruler of India was twenty-five times greater than the income of King James I of Great Britain (Pearson, 52). The Ottoman Turks attacked Vienna in 1529 and 1683.

But a change was coming. In the early sixteenth century, from their peripheral position, European traders, explorers, conquerors, missionaries, and colonists began venturing out over the world. By 1800, Europeans controlled 35 percent of the world's land area, having established permanent settlements on all the continents except Australia and Antarctica (Parry 1961, 162). Aided by African slavers, they had been bringing slaves to their new possessions in the western hemisphere for three centuries. The British had become the dominant power on the Indian subcontinent. China's power had dissipated, declining steadily from its peak; by the middle of the nineteenth century, Europeans were dictating Chinese policy. By 1914, Europeans controlled 84 percent of the world's land area. By 1920, they controlled the Muslim heartland in the Middle East. Great Britain and its empire were the heart of the international economic system. Europe was responsible for almost two-thirds of world trade and an even greater part of world investment (Stevenson).

The European conquest transformed not just Europe's position among world powers; it transformed the world. It encouraged or forced vast migrations, mixing populations and creating new peoples as it diminished or destroyed others. In doing so, it changed, created, or destroyed languages. It made Christianity a global religion. It brought the slave trade to an industrial level and then, under the leadership of Great Britain and with the assistance of the United States, suppressed it. It helped create and then spread the modern state and democracy. It created routes for trade, avenues of commerce, and lines of communication binding the earth. Following its own revolutions in thinking—religious, scientific, political, and, above all, moral—the European conquest challenged traditional thought, destroying customary social organizations, opening new human possibilities and closing others. The humans, animals, plants, diseases, and artifacts the Europeans transported around the world changed climates, landscapes, and daily lives (Calloway). As one historian has noted, "the great going-out over the sea did not change everything, but it changed everything it touched" (Brady, 156, 118). The conquest was the beginning of modern history.

Europeans conquered with trade, arms, and ideas, the latter at first largely religious, then later secular. Trapped on the edge of the Eurasian landmass, with their backs to the sea, blocked from the riches of Asia by the great Muslim empires of the Middle East, Europeans faced the ocean and set sail. In 1415, the Portuguese took Ceuta on the North African Coast, which Muslims had taken from the Byzantines in 710, and then ranged slowly south along the African coast in search of a passage to the Indian Ocean and the lost and fabulously wealthy Christian kingdom of Prester John, thought to exist somewhere beyond the Muslim lands. Developing their comparative advantage in ocean sailing, first acquired through fishing the Atlantic, the Portuguese contrived techniques of sailing and navigating that made possible these long trips of great risk and hardship. Eventually, Vasco da Gama rounded the Cape of Good Hope at the southernmost tip of Africa, reaching India in 1498. This gave the Portuguese direct access to the wealth and trade of India and the spice islands, allowing them to compete with Venice and other Italian cities that had acted as middlemen between Europe and Asia.

The Portuguese had direct access, but they had little or nothing to offer in trade that was of particular interest to the wealthier, more sophisticated people (who did not include the mythical Prester John) they encountered on the far side of Africa. If they had proceeded simply according to the terms of trade, the Portuguese would have failed. Instead, they employed force. Their oceangoing vessels turned out to be good gun platforms, allowing them to control the sea and threaten ports and their protecting forts. The Portuguese did trade but within the context of a protection racket: their military force created a threat, which they then used to extort tribute (fees and taxes) from those they threatened in return for not carrying out their threat (Pearson, 79). This was the same approach used by the Mongols and other nomads when they had control of the overland trade routes across the steppes. (It is also the business strategy of contemporary North Korea.) The protection racket was an efficient political–economic model because it allowed the Portuguese imperial enterprise to pay for itself. Those who manned and led the Portuguese forces paid themselves through plunder. The Portuguese aspired to a monopoly of the spice trade, but ultimately Portugal, a small state, had too little power to dominate Indian Ocean trade. Portuguese military superiority was neither great enough nor sustainable. Others, principally the Dutch and English, followed and supplanted the Portuguese.

The Dutch, English, and Spanish also headed west, of course, across the Atlantic in search of Asia, but instead they found the western hemisphere. Conquest for wealth and glory and to spread Christianity motivated the Spanish. The English shared these motivations at first, but over time trade and settlement became more important to them. Commerce was most important to the Dutch, their settlements being little more than trading posts. The French, when they joined the hunt, fixed on trade and conversion of the natives to Catholicism. Their settlement of North America was sparse. In the Caribbean, the French and British grew sugar, finding it immensely profitable, and expanded the African slave trade to feed the beast of sugar production, just as the Portuguese did in Brazil. Overall, the Portuguese carried about half of all slaves taken to the western hemisphere, the British about a quarter. The Spanish used forced indigenous labor to extract silver and gold from the lands they took. Except for the Spanish, who relied largely on force, the Europeans used trade and war together to extend their grasp over every land they touched.

Two examples, one in the early history of Europe, another from the latter stages of the European conquest, make clear the interaction of trade and war. In addition to raiding the coasts of Ireland and England, the Vikings moved from the Baltic into Eastern Europe. This area did not provide targets of plunder like the monasteries and coastal towns of the British Isles, but its rivers were channels of trade leading into the wealthy Muslim world. During the ninth century, the Vikings used force to gain control of the rivers and the territory around them. They then grew wealthy exchanging silver from the Muslim world for the furs and timber extracted by the labor of those they had conquered or selling these laborers themselves as slaves. Their increased wealth meant increased power to protect their trade routes and to extract labor from subordinate peoples. This early activity of fighting and trading gradually led to the development of the Kievan Rus state, the forerunner of modern Russia, as the best way to organize coercion and protect commerce. The state in this case, and generally (as we see in the next chapter), was a development from the original processes of trade and war. It came about because centralized control of the means of coercion and extraction (taxes or forced labor, for example) proved over the long run more efficient and effective, and more powerful, than the more decentralized organization of tribes.

The second example of conquest through coercion and commerce better shows their reciprocal relationship and does so on a global scale. When the British East India Company was first extending its influence in India it was at a commercial disadvantage because the demand for Indian cotton textiles was so strong in Europe. This demand gave the Indian textile producers leverage. Victory at the battle of Plassey (1757) increased the company's control of territory at the expense of the local rulers and the French, Britain's great imperial rival. With this increased control, the company was able to impose a monopoly on the textile producers and trade. This monopoly increased its revenues, which financed its continuing expansion in India, with the coercive aid of its army of sepoys (native Indian soldiers) serving under British officers. By one accounting (Findlay and O'Rourke, 76, 274–75), the wealth produced by the company was also critical in financing British efforts during the Seven Years' War or, as it was known in the American colonies, the French and Indian War (1756–63), the first global war, which ended with Britain taking control of France's North American territory.

The capture of Havana during this first global war demonstrates the reciprocal relationship between war and trade. The city was a critical port in Spain's military and commercial empire. Losing almost half the troops that besieged the city, most to diseases like yellow fever, the British finally captured it, along with a horde of gold and silver and Spain's Caribbean fleet. Having conquered the city, the British were too weak in men to hold it, but local Spanish merchants saw great advantages in trading within the British empire and so cooperated with the new imperial power. These merchants, their British counterparts, and the empire as a whole profited from the seizure of Havana, which, like the previous examples, illustrates how "war and trade were complementary ways of gaining control of what belonged to others" (Anderson, 497–502; Brady, 142).

War and trade as means of acquiring are as old as humanity. We now call the version of these practices followed by the European powers in the seventeenth and eighteenth centuries "mercantilism." The assumption of mercantilism was that just as one man could not gain without causing another to lose, so one nation could not gain without causing another nation to lose (Viner, 8–9). The total sum of wealth was static; the task of an individual or a nation was to get as much of it as possible. On these assumptions, it made sense to use force to gain monopoly control of an area and invest the increased revenue to create greater force. Or it made sense to trade and gain enough wealth to build strong military forces to gain monopoly control of an area and protect one's commerce so that one could increase one's wealth. Power created plenty; plenty created power. In some times or places one preceded the other or was more important than the other, but they worked together to build European power.

Mercantilism had a shorter life than the imperialism it helped inspire. In the later stages of European imperialism, Europeans no longer generally assumed that one party's gain had to be another's loss or that the total amount of wealth was static. Generally, liberal views prevailed, which held that wealth could grow for all, domestically and globally, and that free trade domestically and internationally was a principal way to grow it. This theory reduced the need to use violence to enforce monopolies of trade, although it created the need for violence or the threat of violence to open markets and, paradoxically, impose free trade. (The origin of these liberal ideas and their connection to imperialism are discussed in the next chapter.) The British began to learn the new lesson about coercion and commerce following the American Revolution, which changed only the political, not the economic, terms of the British relationship with the colonies that became the United States. The British invested heavily in the United States after the revolution because they profited handsomely, as did the Americans, from these investments.

The Conquest of South America

While the reciprocal relationship between trade and war explains a good deal about the European conquest, especially in its early stages, it does not explain everything. The Spanish conquest of Mexico demonstrates how European imperialism differed from other kinds. Spain was the major European power in the sixteenth century. It had resources and military skills developed in various European dynastic wars and in the reconquest of the Iberian peninsula from the Moors. This fighting also produced a class of warrior-gentlemen or, more accurately perhaps, "down-at-heel swordsmen," proud and hungry for fame and fortune. It was these men, the conquistadores, actually a mere handful of them, who got Spain its Mexican empire. Never had so few conquered so many in so short a time. How did they manage it? They had military technology—guns, horses, armor, and steel swords—superior to that of the indigenous forces, but they had relatively little of it. The Spaniards who conquered the Aztecs in what is now Mexico had initially thirteen muskets, fourteen cannon, and sixteen horses. The greatest impact of the horses may have been psychological, as they were new to the continent, but even as the shock the beasts inflicted wore off, the tactical and strategic advantages they offered persisted. Not only were the horses faster than Amerindians on foot, but they raised the Spanish above the natives, allowing them to slash and stab their armorless opponents. Following skilled and ruthless leadership, the Spanish were fiercely determined. They had to conquer or die. They also fought to kill, whereas the Aztecs fought to take prisoners, whom they would later sacrifice. The Spanish were also inspired by their religion, which had led them to retake the Iberian peninsula from the Muslim Moors and now motivated them to take a new land. And they had the help of native peoples whom the Aztecs had exploited for years. Finally, the Spanish brought with them infectious diseases unknown in the western hemisphere, and these devastated the local population (Parry 1961, 54–55; Findlay and O'Rourke, 159–60; Elliott, 24–35).

The epidemics gave Amerindians no time to recover because of the scale and the frequency with which they occurred. They ripped apart the fabric of Amerindian social life; disrupted economic activity, leading to hunger and in some cases famine; deprived the Amerindians of leaders; disrupted the oral process of transmitting the lore, techniques, and traditions by which they sustained their way of life; and, in general, demoralized the survivors, calling into question all that they had known and lived by. Some were driven to convert to Christianity. During the conquest, Europeans did try to aid the Amerindians, for both humanitarian and self-interested reasons. When the practices became known, some inoculated or vaccinated the Amerindians. None of these efforts prevented the large-scale destruction of the population, however (Calloway, 38–40).

Disease was an important part of the European conquest of the western hemisphere, not just of Mexico. European-born epidemics (as well as animals and trade goods) reached Amerindians before the Europeans did. The Incas suffered from Spanish diseases before they suffered from Spanish swords. Shortly before the first English colonists arrived in what is now Massachusetts, epidemics originating in contact with European traders, explorers, or fishermen had killed thousands of Amerindians in New England. Such epidemics continued their work through the seventeenth and eighteenth centuries. Each wave of disease killed half, two-thirds, or even more of a native population.

Epidemic disease was certainly a cause of native weakness in the western hemisphere, as technological advantage was a cause of European strength in many places. We should not overemphasize, however, either disease or technology as an explanation of the global European conquest. Disease did not help the Europeans in Asia, since the Asians they encountered were immune to germs the Europeans carried. In Africa, the Caribbean, and some parts of Asia, tropical diseases worked against the Europeans, as in the case of the siege of Havana. In Africa, they effectively barred European penetration. This changed only in the later stages of imperialism during the nineteenth century, with the use of quinine, for example, to protect against malaria and, in the Caribbean, with the identification of mosquitos as the carriers of yellow fever and steps to control them. Europeans, then, were able eventually to control 84 percent of the world's land area, even though not all of that area had been as deeply affected by disease as the western hemisphere. Moreover, although all inhabitants of the western hemisphere were susceptible to European disease, the Spanish were not able to extend their control to all parts of South America with equal speed or ease. The Aztecs succumbed quickly; the Incas, less so. The first two Spanish efforts to conquer them failed. Areas surrounding the Aztec and Inca empires were difficult to subdue. In some cases, it took the Spanish decades or longer to establish control. And throughout these efforts they had the same technological advantage, although not always the same success.

Considering the causes of this variation allows us a better understanding of the European conquest and what made the European conquest distinctive. Although disease and weapons technology feature in many contemporary accounts (e.g., Headrick, Diamond), it is important to remember the human attitudes and intentions that shape action in the circumstances these powerful agents may create. Some of the variation in the Spanish conquest of the Americas, for example, resulted simply from what the Spanish desired. Initially, they were principally after gold and silver, not land on which to farm, as the settlers along the eastern seaboard of North America sought. The Spanish therefore focused on areas that supplied mineral wealth. Exploring south from Panama, they came into contact with the Inca empire, saw evidence of its wealth, and made it a target. Their desire to convert the indigenous people and their need for land on which to raise cattle later led them to seize land without mineral wealth. Their need for slaves prompted them to raid in territories they did not need to control. So although in the means of coercion the Spanish had technological superiority, and in disease a powerful unintended ally, their intentions shaped the pattern and timing of their conquests. These intentions, in turn, derived from certain attitudes about the world or a distinctive way of dealing with the problems that confront all human beings.

Part of a rebellion against Spanish control, the siege of Cuzco (May 1536–March 1537), in which perhaps as many as 100,000 Incas sought to take the city from about 190 Spaniards and a few thousand Amerindian allies (Hemming, 185–86), reveals these other elements of the conquest. The Inca siege failed for several reasons. The Inca leader, Manco, may have made some tactical and strategic errors in his management of the campaign. Horses gave the Spanish the ability to conduct quick raids into the countryside to gather food, allowing them to withstand the siege. Amerindian allies also helped sustain the Spanish. When the Incas captured a post overlooking Cuzco, the Spanish launched a desperate counterattack to retake it, which succeeded. At another desperate moment, when everything seemed to turn against them, the Spanish attacked the besiegers. In these engagements the new tactics and weapons of the Amerindians extracted a high cost from the Spanish, but they held on. They displayed fighting sprit, no doubt born of desperation, and a courage and daring admirable in itself, if not for the ends it served. The siege broke, to some degree because the Incas were discouraged but more because they needed to tend to their crops if they were to feed themselves and their families in the year ahead. Most of the Inca army were conscripts, not professional soldiers. In addition to their other advantages, the Spanish were the vanguard of increasingly wealthy states and empires that could generate and project significant power even thousands of miles across the Atlantic (Elliott, 9–10). As the rebellion and siege developed, the Spanish leader in the coastal lowlands heard of it and called on the rest of the Spanish new world empire for assistance. Reinforcements came from Mexico, Panama, and even Hispaniola (modern-day Haiti and the Dominican Republic), among other places. The Incas had only their own resources to call on (Hemming, 189–220).

The Spanish had another advantage. As both a military force and an instrument of political power, they were more cohesive than the Incas. The support that came from the rest of the empire reflected a generally held sense of common purpose among the Spanish. While the conquistadores feuded and competed among themselves, they did manage to work together against the Incas. In addition, the Spaniards were accustomed to working in a military structure that established not only clear lines of subordination among officers but also the expectation that subordinate officers, based on their skill, experience, and personal characteristics, as well as their social status, would over time rise in rank or in emergencies take command. This understanding of rank and subordination gave the Spanish forces resilience. If a Spanish commander fell in battle or was otherwise incapacitated, the next ranking officer could take charge and the Spanish could continue to fight as a cohesive force.

The Inca empire, by contrast, had grown to its immense size only in the hundred years or so before the Spanish appeared. It consisted of diverse tribes not all successfully integrated. The material rewards of the empire were unevenly shared. The supposed divinity of the Inca rulers was an article of faith only among the Incas themselves; the idea was foreign to the other tribes they ruled. Leadership was restricted to the royal family, but the principle of succession was not clear. The result was succession by civil war. One such war had just ended as the Spanish invaded. Hence the Incas who confronted the Spanish were weakened not only by smallpox but also by the casualties and fatigue of their internal conflict. The Inca army was hierarchical, organized in subordinate units under a professional officer corps, but the status distinction between the officers and the conscript farmers was great. The Incas often fought bravely, but their forces tended to disintegrate once their leaders had been killed. Over the long years of the conquest, the discipline and cohesion of professional or regular European troops, constantly drilled in weapons and tactics, often proved superior to the indigenous forces they faced.

The Incas innovated both technologically and tactically to deal with the Spanish threat, but the social and cultural constraints on their cohesion affected their ability to deploy new tactics successfully. They developed the *bola*, weights attached to lengths of animal tendons that when hurled could wrap around the legs of horses and bring them down. The Incas also dug traps to ensnare horses or diverted rivers and streams to flood fields, mire horses, and reduce their mobility. Virtually invincible on flat ground, the Spanish were vulnerable on terrain disadvantageous to their horses or which gave the natives cover or other tactical advantage. Indeed, the Incas avoided battle in the field when they could, instead ambushing the Spanish in mountain canyons by pushing boulders down on them. Using this technique, the

Incas destroyed several separate relief columns sent from the lowlands to relieve the besieged Spanish in Cuzco (Headrick; Hemming). The Incas also acquired and used Spanish weapons, particularly swords and horses, from killed or captured Spaniards. Still, these innovations and forced technology transfers were of little use to the Incas for two reasons. First, the Spanish conquest happened quickly enough that Incas had little time to develop and perfect the innovations or to become as accomplished mounted fighters as the invaders were. Second, the transferred items of technology were too few and were used within the traditional Inca tactical schemes, which reflected Inca social and political structures, limiting their effectiveness.

The strengths and weaknesses of the Spanish and indigenous forces are better understood if we consider a failure of the Spanish conquest. To the south of the Incas lived the Araucanians or Mapuche, hunter-gatherers who also practiced slash-and-burn agriculture. They were a tribal people, organized by kinship, who had no government and, at the time of first contact with the Spanish, less central military and political organization than the Incas. They were also much less wealthy. Their poverty meant that the Spanish had less incentive to control them; their bellicosity raised the cost of enslaving them. These disincentives in part explain the Spanish failure to conquer the Araucanians. The lack of success resulted also, and perhaps more, from the same kinds of factors that explain the outcome of the Spanish-Inca confrontation. In their conflict with the Spanish, the Araucanians had the same technological and tactical disadvantages as the Incas, or perhaps even greater ones. They had greater cohesion, however, since they were bound by kinship and not conquest. As hunter-gatherers they could live off the land in a way that the Incas could not or, using slash-and-burn techniques to create new fields, rapidly establish new agricultural resources if they had to cede territory to the Spanish. This made burning established cropland, a tactic the Spanish used against the Aztecs and other Europeans used repeatedly against indigenous people, less effective. The population density of the Araucanians was much less than that of the Incas or Aztecs, which meant that they were less susceptible to infectious diseases.

The Araucanians' way of life gave them a mobility and resilience that matched or exceeded that of the Spanish and gave them time to adapt to the Spanish way of war, which they did with some effectiveness. Inferior in the open to the Spanish, like all indigenous people at the time, the Araucanians avoided battles and instead raided and ambushed, often attacking at night.

They learned to use terrain disadvantageous to horses, greatly diminishing the Spanish advantage. When they could not avoid battle on open ground, they used a tactical formation (pikes in front, backed by archers) similar to what had developed in Europe as a way to deal with cavalry. They found ways to use captured Spanish weapons to improve their own, and they developed new weapons, including a lasso device, to counter Spanish horsemen. Their mobility and resilience and the disincentives they presented to Spanish conquest gave the Araucanians time to learn how to breed horses and use them effectively in battle. The pasturelands they inhabited gave them a resource that made this adaptation possible. The Araucanians created a stalemate with the Spanish that consisted of each side raiding and trading across the river that separated areas of Spanish and Araucanian control (Headrick, 115–23; Elliott, 39).

In sum, the rapid Spanish conquest in the western hemisphere depended on their ability to direct superior military tactics and technology against a people weakened by disease and internal warfare. The Spanish were fortunate or, as they might have said, blessed in their Aztec and Inca enemies. In different degrees, both native empires were centralized but socially and spiritually fragile. The fortune of the Spanish in this regard is clear when we consider their less successful efforts against the Araucanians and similarly organized indigenous peoples. Against all their enemies, effective Spanish use of tactics, technology, and good fortune depended on superior Spanish social and military cohesion, which at the same time allowed for and even glorified individual initiative and responsibility (Elliott, 8, 4, 42; Parry 1981, 19, 31). This was a distinctive characteristic of all Euro-American imperialism and increasingly set it apart from other kinds (except perhaps for that of the ancient world, the spirit of which was reviving in sixteenth-century Europe). Christianity and religious zeal united, motivated, and fortified the Spanish, but it was not thought incompatible with great martial virtue. The emphasis on personal initiative and glory caused some infighting harmful to the Spanish cause but on balance did more good than harm. The drive to amass personal wealth was a powerful motive for the conquest.

The Conquest of North America

In addition to their activities in Central and South America, the Spanish explored and settled in the southeast and southwest of what is now the United States. They established outposts at Saint Augustine, Florida, in

1565 and at Santa Fe, New Mexico, in 1607. The Spanish presence in these areas, especially in Florida, did not produce the results that the French and the British attained farther north. Starting from two tiny settlements along the coast in the early seventeenth century, the British presence increased dramatically. In the eighteenth century, Germans came in large numbers, perhaps as many as 90,000. From 1760 to 1775, "221,500 immigrants [came] to the British colonies in North America," including large numbers of Protestant Irish, Scots, English, and Germans. By 1790, there were nearly 4 million inhabitants in what had become the United States. Thousands of people lived in the territories west of the Appalachian mountains. This population growth and movement, and the conflict it generated, displaced native populations, as disease continually decreased their numbers (Calloway, 144).

Rather than removing the natives through settlement and war, the French tended to work with them. They established their influence and control principally through trade in beaver skins, although they did put more work into converting the Amerindians to Christianity than the English did, which may reflect a difference between Catholic and Protestant theology (see chapter two). To facilitate the fur trade, they set up forts and trading posts down the Saint Lawrence River, around the Great Lakes, and in the Mississippi valley. Until they lost their North American empire as a result of the French and Indian War, the French ran what one historian has called a "multicultural confederation" (Anderson, 742). They used diplomacy, trade, and fear of the encroaching land-hungry English to form alliances with most of the tribes in the areas they claimed. The French posed less of a threat to the Amerindians than the British, since they did not seize their land, or much of it. The French approach was to negotiate differences to keep the beaver furs moving to Europe, where demand seemed insatiable. The French used their military force to aid their Amerindian allies, especially against the powerful, expansionist Iroquois confederacy, but the French North American empire rested more on trade and conversion than on military force.

The French desire for fur may seem more benign in its consequences than the English craving for land (the English, of course, also sought furs), but it was not, for two reasons, both of which show how trade aided conquest. First, the French traded manufactures and alcohol for fur skins. Both of these trade items disrupted the Amerindian way of life, as the trade itself did, apparently even on occasion leading Amerindians to hunt beaver at the expense of their traditional farming, increasing the uncertainty of their food supply. More commonly, the trade, which gave the Amerindians axes, metal hoes, mirrors, needles, various kinds of woven cloth, and even pewter dishes, lace, and glassware, brought them into the Atlantic economy and made them dependent on a larger world that they did not understand and over which they had no control. It reduced them in a sense to the status of European peasants, but without the legal and customary protection that those peasants enjoyed, at least in principle. Beads manufactured in Europe in time replaced the shells Amerindians had traditionally used for wampum (Calloway, 46), as much of the "traditional" cloth one found in Africa in the twentieth century was actually produced in Europe. Desire for manufactured goods even led to loss of land because Amerindians traded land for European goods. Thomas Jefferson once proposed trading with the Amerindians to get them in debt so that they would have no way to pay off the debts except by selling their land (Jefferson, 1118).

The fur trade abetted imperialism in another way, too, by increasing conflict among the Amerindians themselves. The most important example of this is the story of the Iroquois confederation. Consisting of five tribes, and later a sixth, located in what is now central and western New York state, the confederation came into existence as a way of dealing with the Europeans appearing to the north and east of the tribes. Early Dutch settlers traded guns for animal pelts, giving the Iroquois an advantage as they continued a tradition of aggressive behavior toward neighboring tribes. Trade and war went hand in hand for these Amerindians, as it did for the Europeans who threatened their empire. The more pelts the Iroquois had to trade, the more guns they received and the more land they could seize from other Amerindians to get more pelts. This was, of course, the same "mercantilist" dynamic driving the European conquest, power making plenty, plenty making power. In the mid-seventeenth century, as part of this dynamic, the Iroquois attacked tribes to their west. Over the next five years or so, they destroyed the Huron (a population of perhaps 30,000 to 40,000), the Erie, and the confederation of tribes known as the Neutral. They later attacked tribes to the east, south, and farther west, as far away as present-day Illinois, with arms supplied by the British, who had supplanted the Dutch and with whom the Iroquois had established an alliance. Eventually, however, the Iroquois experienced a kind of imperial overreach. Exhausted, and confronted with an alliance consisting of the remnants of the tribes they had destroyed and others united with French sponsorship and support, the confederation was torn by disagreements between Francophile, Anglophile, and neutralist factions. After some time, however, the factions managed to fashion a compromise, and toward the end of the seventeenth century the confederation reached a peace agreement with the French, without giving up their alliance with the English. This allowed the Iroquois to play the two European powers against each other. In doing so, they also served as middlemen in the trade between other Amerindians and the Europeans, while turning their aggression toward tribes to the south (Anderson, 13–15; Waldman, 113–14).

Just as "mercantilism" is important in explaining the Iroquois confederation, so did religion play a role in the Iroquois story analogous to the role it played in the European conquest. The Iroquois confederation was built on a long-established spiritual and ritual foundation. Before the five tribes were a confederation to deal with the growing European presence, they had been the League of Peace and Power, designed to stop conflict between themselves. The religion of the league prescribed rituals and gift giving to take the place of retributive killing. The league's religion did not determine only its domestic policy or the conduct of its members toward each other. It determined the league's foreign policy as well. The Iroquois believed that all people should be members of their league. "People who refused to heed the Good News as allies or dependents . . . could only be dealt with as enemies. The Iroquois believed that war against such recalcitrant nations was not only just but necessary, because conquest and forcible subjection to the Great League offered the only remaining way that they, too, could find the path to peace" (Anderson, 13). This desire to bring peace to the world led to almost nonstop hostilities as the Iroquois set out to convert everyone. Religion not only turned the Iroquois into experienced warriors; it gave them cohesion. It also prepared them institutionally, so to speak, to develop a political confederation to deal with the new world of conflict that the Europeans brought. In these ways, Iroquois religion functioned on a smaller scale in a way similar to Islam and Christianity in Arab or European empires.

The Iroquois, however, were not prepared for Christianity, a religion that also had universalist, if otherwise to them odd, claims. The French brought with them missionaries, Jesuits, who had their own Good News and worked not only among the Amerindians allied with the French but also with members of the Iroquois confederation. The missionaries succeeded in converting some of these members, particularly Mohawks, who left their traditional areas and settled near the Saint Lawrence River or in other mission villages. All the tribes in the confederation felt the effect of missionary activity, and this further factionalized and weakened them (Anderson, 14). Something similar occurred among the Amerindians in contact with the Puritans. Some of these converts became intermediaries between Puritans and Amerindians; many moved into "praying villages." During King Philip's War they became victims of both the Amerindians, who saw them as traitors, and the Puritans, who did not trust them.

The Iroquois were not, of course, the only Amerindians affected by Christianity. Conversion split several tribes into factions, including the Huron, Oneida, and Delaware. Conversion changed religious beliefs, but it also meant social change, since missionaries insisted that the converts conform to European ideas of gender relations (some tribes were more gender egalitarian than Europeans) and sexual and marital conduct, for example. Altogether, such changes amounted to "social revolution and cultural disintegration." Conversion had political and geopolitical consequences as well. Some Amerindians, converts or not, tried to manipulate the religious factionalism in their tribes. The Abenaki remained loyal to the French at least in part because they remained loyal to their adopted Catholicism (Calloway, 76, 87–90).

Of the factors involved in the European conquest of North America, missionary activity was certainly not the most important. But it was powerful because it did not work in isolation from trade, war, and disease. For example, hunting was not just an economic activity for the Amerindians, a way to stay alive; it had religious significance. Amerindian desire for European artifacts and alcohol led them to hunt more as a commercial activity than as a way of life, as the missionaries worked to undermine traditional Amerindian religious practices, many connected to traditional ways of hunting. This increased the "social revolution and cultural disintegration," which was also occurring as the failure of their shamans to deal with the new diseases caused some Amerindians to seek the aid of Christianity. The European conquest of North America succeeded because of the reciprocal relationship not just of trade and war but of trade, war, religion, and disease. War and disease killed many; trade and Christianity together subverted most others.

Warfare between North American Amerindians and Europeans changed as their confrontation continued. In the southeast, in the early sixteenth century, the Spanish confronted Amerindians who lived in large towns and massed warriors in the field. Spanish technological and tactical advantages, again largely swords and horses, made that an ineffective approach, so the Amerindians changed their tactics. They learned to disperse and ambush. This pattern recurred, especially as guns became fully integrated into European armies. The Amerindians used what the Europeans called a skulking way of warfare, which included ambushes, raids, and attacks on civilians and their property (Grenier, 32; Calloway 104–5). As Amerindians acquired guns in trade or from one European ally or another, they too integrated them into their way of war and learned to use them effectively. Amerindians in the western hemisphere did stand and fight, as we saw in the case of the Incas, and they often inflicted significant casualties on Europeans. But generally fighting Europeans in the open field was not to their advantage. So the Amerindians "skulked." The Europeans responded to skulking by targeting Amerindian villages and crops. When Amerindians would not meet the Europeans in the field but melted into the woods, they left these resources, and often their women and children, vulnerable to European attack. Not being able to draw the Amerindians to battle, the Europeans had to destroy what sustained them and allowed them to resist. Often, Europeans would wait until harvest time to do this, since the Amerindians would thus face starvation without any time to recover. Sometimes Europeans targeted resources and noncombatants because it appeared more cost effective. Militias could do this work, for example, sparing professionals for more difficult military tasks. As composed largely of the farmers most exposed to Amerindian skulking, militia forces had personal as well as strategic reasons to undertake the work. On other occasions, attacking resources and noncombatants was explicitly an effort to annihilate the Amerindians rather than to compel them to come to terms (Grenier, 141–42, 195; Calloway, 99–100, 104–6; Taylor, 39, 56).

Both the military interaction and the outcome of Euro-Amerindian conflict depended on more than tactics and technology. Social structure, beliefs, and practices were important as well. Based on extended kinship ties, Amerindian society in eastern North America was different from what the Spanish encountered in Central and South America. The Amerindian tribes of North America were less stratified by wealth and status than European settler society. Authority among the Amerindians was decentralized and more personal than among Europeans. A governor of a colony had authority because of the position he held, whatever his personal accomplishments or merit. Certainly, poor performance, self-aggrandizement, or political ineptitude undermined a governor's authority, but the authority of office could sustain the authority of the person holding it, despite his personal failings. Among the Amerindians, personal merit had a more direct and immediate connection to authority, or the lack of it. The decentralized, personal nature of Amerindian society affected how the Amerindians fought. For example, battle was a way to show individual prowess, and an Amerindian warrior could demonstrate that prowess by taking trophies, such as prisoners or scalps. Once that was done, his personal objectives satisfied, the Amerindian warrior might retire from the field. The larger band of which he was a part might also think the fight over, once sufficient casualties had been inflicted on the enemy or prisoners taken either for adoption into the tribe or to be ritually tortured to death to assuage the grief of those in the tribe who had lost kin in the conflict. In October 1774, in defense of their lands, Shawnee attacked an army of Virginians at Point Pleasant, in what is now West Virginia. The Amerindians made 40 percent of the Virginians casualties, suffering many fewer of their own. To the Amerindians, this was a victory, but the Virginians did not withdraw. They regrouped and pressed on, eventually forcing the Shawnee to accept a treaty in which they gave up land. The Shawnee experienced this different approach to war sixteen years later when they and their Miami allies ambushed and badly mauled an American force, which withdrew. The Amerindians did not pursue the retreating Americans because they "were content with their victories and had left the field to celebrate" (Grenier, 151, 196). For the Americans, however, this initial defeat was only the beginning of the war. The characteristic ways of Amerindian warriors and warfare also made them difficult allies from the European point of view. The Amerindians did not fit easily, or at all, into European command-and-control structures and, again, might see a successful battle as the end of the war. Many European officers discounted the Amerindians, but those who understood them could use their unsurpassed knowledge of the land and their mobility to good advantage. Generally speaking, the Amerindians fought seasonally, for limited or personal objectives, and thought of war in terms of battles. (On these last two points, the Iroquois, as noted, were an exception.) The Europeans, particularly with the experience of the religious and then the dynastic wars of the sixteenth through eighteenth centuries as their touchstone, were willing to fight more continually, pursued political and strategic objectives, as well as personal ones, and thought in terms of campaigns—series of battles—to achieve their objectives. Like the Europeans, Amerindians fought for gain and glory but lacked the Europeans' more centralized social and political structure. The Europeans had the economic and bureaucratic means to make sustained warfare possible, thanks to their emerging nation-state structures, which were in turn the product of years and years of warfare in Europe. (For more on this development, see chapter two.) The Europeans succeeded against the Amerindians of both North and South America, we might say, because they managed to combine the personal initiative of the former with the centralization of the latter.

As the exception of the Iroquois indicates, it is possible to overstate the differences in Amerindian and European ways of war in North America. In practice, the Amerindians and Europeans adapted to the ways the other fought. The Amerindians incorporated guns into their way of war. They also learned to fight for new reasons and with greater intensity, as the commercialization of hunting increased the desire for land and European weapons increased Amerindian firepower. Amerindians had always taken some captives as slaves, but supplying the demand for slave labor in the colonies, in order to purchase more weapons, artifacts, and alcohol, was another new incentive for conflict. For their part, the Europeans sometimes adopted Amerindian dress (e.g., moccasins) and tried to emulate skulking. They armed some units with rifles to be fired from concealed positions or taught soldiers to fire lying down, or to disperse into the trees when ambushed to return fire, and modified their uniforms. The development of colonial ranger detachments was an institutional expression of this adaptation. Rangers were smaller military units, lightly armed and mobile, which carried out scouting and raiding operations in support of larger military units or on their own, often in an effort to deal with the Amerindians in a cost-efficient and more effective way. Rogers's Rangers is the best known of these units, and its raid on the Amerindian village of St. Francis in 1759 the most famous ranger operation. The forests of North America made light infantry more valuable; British forces came to include more of them than they would have in Europe. Other organizational adaptations included armed boatmen to protect supplies as they traveled on North America's many rivers and lakes, vital transport links in the absence of roads. For the same reasons, Europeans used the Amerindian birch canoe, a remarkably well-designed mode of transportation for people and supplies. Finally, because of the expense of maintaining troops in North America, the British relied more heavily on auxiliaries, both local militias and Amerindians, than they would have in Europe (Anderson, 410–12; Russell, 645).

Another reason that the difference between Amerindian and European means of war was not as great as one might think is that British officers, for example, had experience of "skulking" or irregular warfare before they got to America. European armies in the eighteenth century used irregular forces, often from the marches or from places in Europe, such as the Balkans, where such warfare was more common, to do many of the tasks rangers performed in North American wars. They scouted, ambushed, raided, foraged, and provided flanking cover for regular forces. Before their service in America, British officers prominent in North American warfare, such as John Forbes and James Wolfe, had studied military writings based on the European experience with irregular forces or had direct experience of irregular warfare in Scotland. Nor were the harsher means of warfare practiced in North America unknown in Europe. While fighting irregular forces in the marches in Ireland and Scotland, for example, British regulars had frequently attacked civilians, burning villages and crops (Russell, 634, 641; Grenier, 93, 102–3; Lee). Despite these similarities, however, irregular or partisan warfare in Europe was peripheral to the main business of forming a battle line in open space and engaging the enemy. Or it was reserved for dealing with those perceived as less civilized—for example, Highlanders or the Irish—who, like the Amerindians in North America, would not stand and fight or who, having stood, refused to admit they had been defeated and continued the struggle in small bands and out-of-the-way places (Russell, 635, 640). In North America as well, European armies formed battle lines or laid siege, but irregular warfare assumed greater importance than in Europe, both in supporting regular armies and as a separate way of dealing with Amerindians. We should also remember that while Europeans could "trade down" to fight in a manner similar to the Amerindians', the Amerindians could not "trade up" and fight like Europeans.

Amerindians were not just trade partners and war allies of the French or the British. They rose against them in defense of their way of life. Perhaps the most important of these resistance movements, especially in the eighteenth century, was the one known as Pontiac's Rebellion (1763–64). The rebellion was loosely organized but widespread. It drew energy from local grievances but also from the distress of disease and famine and a generalized discontent with policies adopted by the British in the aftermath of their victory in the Seven Years' War. The British did not stop settlers encroaching on Amerindian land, yet they did stop giving gifts to the Amerindians and curtailed trade, especially in alcohol and guns. The Amerindians liked none of this. The resistance movement ultimately encompassed tribes from the Delaware valley to the Mississippi River and from Michigan through Ohio. One reason that so many different tribes were able to combine is that they all became inspired by a religious movement that originated among the Delaware. Like Islamists in the twentieth century, the movement preached that the Amerindians could only be saved by a somewhat selective return to their ancestral ways. They should give up alcohol, contact with Europeans, and relearn ancient ways of war and living (Dowd, 97–98, 112). (What they embraced as "traditional ways" were in fact to some extent innovations, like the later "Ghost Dance" adopted by native Americans at the end of the nineteenth century. This too is similar to the innovative traditionalism of twentieth-century Muslim writers and politicians like Sayyid Qutb and Ayatollah Khomeini.)

In April 1763, the Ottawa, under the war chief Pontiac, laid siege to Detroit. Eventually, about 900 warriors from six different nations joined the attackers. As news of the siege of Detroit spread among the Amerindians, others arose and attacked more forts. Many of the forts and outposts that the Amerindians attacked fell, but the three most important—Niagara, Detroit, and Pittsburgh—managed to hold out. The British commander in North America, Jeffery Amherst, authorized his forces to give smallpox-infested blankets to the Amerindians and to kill Amerindian captives. But above all he counted on the fractious ways of the Amerindians and their limited logistic capacities to blunt the uprising as he prepared a more effective response. His successor, Thomas Gage, carried out punitive expeditions in 1764 and authorized treaty negotiations, facilitated by William Johnson, an established British-Amerindian intermediary. These efforts, along with Amerindian exhaustion, brought this phase of indigenous resistance to a close (Anderson, 535–46).

These patterns were repeated in the later phases of the American conquest of North America. The Spanish brought horses and guns to the western hemisphere. When from the late seventeenth century, through trade or theft, horses reached the Amerindians living on or in the vicinity of the great central plains of North America, they transformed Amerindian life. It became much easier to hunt buffalo, and the greater extraction of that resource from their surrounding world made much richer those Amerindians who mastered the skill of hunting while riding. It also led to competition among the tribes for access to buffalo and, eventually, to almost incessant warfare. French traders provided guns to the plains Amerindians in return for hides, which initiated a competition for weapons and increased the Amerindians' ability to kill not only buffalo but each other. "By stealing from the weak, the stronger grew still stronger in people, horses, and firearms at the expense of the losers" (Taylor, 48). In a version of the imperial competition that led the English, Spanish, and French to the western hemisphere and eventually transformed the lives of the Plains Amerindians, power led to plenty and plenty to more power, as the Amerindians who won traded captives and hides with the French for yet more guns. The competition and warfare among the Amerindians led to some groups, for example the Comanche on the southern plains, becoming dominant. It also made the Amerindians effective warriors, as the Europeans' incessant warfare had honed their martial skills. As Americans moved west, they found the Plains Amerindians formidable opponents. Eventually, however, Amerindian resistance was overcome. As had Europeans earlier in the conquest, the U.S. military adapted some of the Amerindians' techniques to combat them, learning them through Amerindian allies. U.S. fighters also eventually got weapons that could be fired more effectively from horseback. The Amerindians acquired these too, but the improved mounted American firepower still removed an initial Amerindian advantage. Disease continued to kill large numbers of Amerindians. At least four epidemics of smallpox struck the Plains Amerindians in the nineteenth century. They also suffered from measles, tuberculosis, cholera, and influenza (Waldman, 190). Perhaps most detrimental to the Amerindians was the decimation of the buffalo by American hunters, a destruction to which the Amerindians contributed, especially once they became part of the European commercial world. Also, the Plains Amerindians were nomads, whose survival on the plains was precarious. In winter, they suffered from lack of food. By contrast, the Americans and their military in the west, the spearpoint of an industrializing and increasingly wealthy nation, had vast resources to draw on. They could supply men campaigning in winter. Once the campaign started, the military pursued the Amerindians until they were exhausted. The Americans also destroyed Amerindian villages and food supplies and killed noncombatants, much as the Amerindians had done in fighting other Amerindians, as the Spanish had done to the Aztecs, and as Caesar's legions had done against the tribes in Gaul.

The Means of Imperial Acquisition

As we have seen, the British used the reciprocal relationship between power and plenty to acquire their empire in India during the eighteenth and early nineteenth centuries, just as the Comanche used it to acquire theirs in the southern plains at roughly the same time. This is less a striking coincidence than simply another example of age-old human practice seen among the Iroquois, the Mongols, and the Portuguese. What distinguished the British and other Europeans from the Comanche and other non-Europeans in the necessary practice of acquisition was the degree to which the former from the early sixteenth century onward condoned and thus freed it, both rationalizing and institutionalizing it. All other ends were subordinate to acquisition (or put another way, church and state were eventually separated). One sees this, for example, in the Spanish conquest. Initial efforts to treat the Amerindians humanely and prevent the slave trade, in which clerics figured prominently, surrendered to the requirements of wealth creation (Elliott, 15, 17, 19). Over time, across the western nations of Europe, rights to property and other legal and political regimes were based on and intended to encourage individual striving. European states came to embody the will and energy of Europe's "rational and industrious," as they extended their power over other Europeans (e.g., the Celtic fringe in Great Britain) and non-Europeans alike. A moral revolution powered empire.

Although Europeans approached the world with a more or less common set of attitudes and eventually institutions, the means they used to conquer varied. In India, more so than in North America, the conquerors used the techniques of regular European warfare: largely infantry forces backed by artillery and cavalry, supported by indigenous allies or auxiliaries, deployed on the open battlefield in search of a decisive victory. The Indians had traditions of bringing large armies into the field and they had significant immovable assets (cities, agricultural areas, industries, skilled workers) to protect, so they met the Europeans in the field. Certainly in the early stages, trade with Europe did not revolutionize the lives of Asians as it did the lives of native North Americans. Europeans had little of interest to offer Asians. Trade gave the Europeans a foothold, but force of arms was the key to the European conquest of Asia until the Industrial Revolution eventually gave the Europeans a commercial advantage, drawing Asians into the European, and then Euro-American, consumer world. Eventually, the British learned to manufacture cloth of superior quality at lower cost than indigenous cloth, even when transported from Great Britain to India. Trade gave Europeans access to India; access led to involvement in Indian politics. "The British won power as participants in Indian power struggles," lending military and political support to one side or the other. In this way, political penetration created the opportunity for political dominance (Marshall, 497). Dominance came through military superiority. This superiority consisted not so much in technology or tactics (except at sea and, with steamships, on rivers). Some of the local rulers had, or could purchase from other Europeans, weapons as good as or superior to those the British possessed, at least into the first decades of the nineteenth century. Indian rulers also hired European officers to transform their militaries along European lines. Skirmishing and raiding by indigenous light cavalry posed many problems for the British. The British commander Arthur Wellesley once said that he would "happily appropriate" captured Indian artillery for use by the British army (Bryant, 444; Duffy, 199; Roy, 677). British military superiority was principally in organization and logistics. These in turn reflected an approach to the world, rationalizing and technological (Parry 1981, 3, 16), not shared by Indians or other non-Europeans.

The British forces that conquered India relied primarily on infantry and artillery. As I show in the next chapter, such forces were the product of a moral, social, economic, intellectual, and political revolution that European warfare had helped generate, if not cause (Ralston, 1–12). In their reliance on cavalry, Indian forces represented a way of life and attitude toward the world that Europeans had left behind. The Indian approach was more personalistic and status-bound than was the British. Indian princes still had to lead their forces in the field; if the prince was killed, the army might disintegrate. Living, he and others held their positions because of who they were rather than their competence as commanders. In the field with large retinues, Indian princes often preferred skirmishing and bribing their opponents to fighting a decisive battle. This is an approach similar to North American Indians counting "coup," or gaining prestige points in battle, rather than land or treasure. Nobles were mounted horsemen, disdaining those who fought on foot, like the French nobility at Agincourt (Keegan), but unlike the petty nobles and striving gentry who led British forces during the empire. The nobles in India resisted change that threatened their status, even when their heavy cavalry tactics proved ineffective against the firepower of disciplined professional infantry. Emphasis on heavy cavalry, which attain their effect in battle by the shock of their engagement with the enemy and not by maneuver, was one reason that Indian forces lacked the articulation into subunits that gave European forces an advantage in maneuver. Once cavalry deliver the shock, they lose cohesion; their fighting dissolves into individual personal combats, dissipating their force, even as it displays individual valor. Personalized rule meant a lack of the institutional and bureaucratic means to extract the revenue necessary to fight in the European style. Lack of money meant lack of drill, training, and professionalism, as well as an inability to sustain campaigns. As the Mughal empire disintegrated, Indian news writers (people who wrote letters for aristocrats and others) accepted British patronage. From them, the British gathered valuable intelligence, as they did from the Indian women with whom they consorted, who provided access as well as information, as did native women in North America (Bryant, 436, 440–41, 445–47, 449, 468; Roy, 667, 680, 682, 688; Marshall, 489, 491–92, 499, 506; Ray, 518; Bayly). As in North America, the clash between British and indigenous forces in India was a clash between a rationalized, "bureaucratic," yet individualistic approach to the world and to warfare on one side and a "heroic," personalistic approach on the other. In both cases, the bureaucrats won. As they did so, and as India became part of the global, now Eurocentric economy, the bureaucratic way transformed Indian society and mores, as it continued to do so in North America. "Everything [in India] had been 'turned upside down'" (Ray, 523, 508–10).

"A world turned upside down" is a vivid description of the consequences of the European conquest, although it does not capture the human toll involved. The conquest produced profound changes because it proceeded not just through force of arms but through trade and ideas. Together, sooner or later, these forces transformed all societies and individuals who came into contact with them. The character of the transformation depended on which of two dominant social organizations the Europeans transformed. In the east, Europeans tended to encounter tributary hierarchical societies, in which dominant coercive force, often legitimated by religious or customary belief, provided some the centralized authority to extract resources from others in return for protection. In North America, Europeans tended to encounter tribal egalitarian societies, constituted by kinship and religious belief, in which decentralized authority was shared, leadership was fluid, based on skill and results, and in which protection came from mutual self-help. Tributary societies were wealthier and more technological than tribal societies, more differentiated by occupation or social position, and more diversified economically. Generally speaking, tributary societies proved harder to conquer than tribal societies, but tribal societies were harder to control when conquered. Tributary societies could muster the resources and technology to defend themselves, making it hard to conquer them, but when victorious, the Europeans could simply put themselves into the place of the previous tribute-gathering authority, continuing the well-established subjugation of the larger population, although under a different official religious sanction. The Spanish conquests of the Aztecs and Incas are good examples of this substitutionary domination, as is the British conquest of India. Tribal societies had a harder time countering European force; often their land could be taken more easily. Kinship ties and tribal life persisted after conquest, however, as long as a sufficient number of the tribe survived their encounter with Europeans. Kinship gave enduring coherence to people; paying tribute did not. Displaced tribes, including the Celtic peoples on the fringes of Great Britain, could maintain an identity, occasionally some independence, and resist. They continue to do so in the early twenty-first century.

Having distinguished tributary and tribal societies, we must of course qualify these distinctions. Some tribal societies approached the tributary model—if not in wealth or technology, at least in the exchange of tribute for protection. The Powhatan confederation in Virginia that the Europeans encountered in the early seventeenth century would be an example. The Iroquois league and later confederation could be offered as another. The Aztecs and the Incas in South America were tributary societies, the latter, like other tributary societies, with a still-evident tribal base. In the Middle East, the Europeans encountered tribal societies, many fortified by Islam. Degrees of centralization and egalitarianism in societies varied both east and west. Some tribal societies developed hereditary chiefdoms, although hereditary rule was more characteristic in what we have described as tributary societies. So many are the qualifications and variations that one might better think of the distinction between tribal and tributary as a rough guide or as designating broad stretches on a continuum that runs from bands of hunter-gatherers, somewhat like the Araucanians, to the states of the Mughal empire.

Alternatively, if we acknowledge all the qualifications necessary when distinguishing tribal and tributary societies and the continuum these qualifications produce, then we might argue that tribal and tributary societies have more in common with each other than either does with the European societies that conquered them. So what made those European societies different? Of course, Europe itself possessed both tribal and tributary societies (the Vikings, Scottish Highlanders; Louis XVI's France, Charles V's Spain), and its tributary states carried out the conquest. But the sociopolitical tributary form common at one point to some of the conquerors and some of the conquered should not disguise what was or became distinctively European. In the next chapter, I consider the question of distinctiveness from the military point of view, but here it is worth emphasizing two ways that the conquering European societies differed from those they conquered. First, Europeans developed an unprecedented "faith in the potentialities of human initiative" to alter and even command the world (Thomas, 661). The conquering Europeans shared "a belief that was gradually gaining ground in sixteenth-century Europe: that it was within the capacity of man to change and improve the world around him" (Elliott, 55; cf. Bakewell, 297). Each authority, everything sacred, all of nature was subject to testing by the restless curiosity and self-aggrandizing manipulation of this initiative. It sought to explore, control, and manipulate its many objects—whether phenomena (the electric charge) or places (the Indian subcontinent). Increasingly, merit was measured not by birth, authority, or law but by what initiative could achieve. Those who took this approach had an advantage in power when they confronted those who did not (Abernethy, 34, 39; Elliott, 33–34). Self-made men, like the conquistadores, made themselves a world.

Of course, even the simplest family group must explore, control, and manipulate its environment in order to survive. What distinguished Europeans was that they, or enough of them, in enough fields of endeavor, prioritized this initiative above everything else. They freed this initiative from all constraint. This freedom is the second way Europeans distinguished themselves from others. Europeans changed the tributary model, making the exchange for tribute include not just protection but also recognition of individual rights, the best protection for individual initiative. The Europeans thus invented the liberal state. Operative as the conquest began, these distinctive and self-reinforcing European ideas increasingly conquered and transformed Europe, even as they conquered and transformed the world, destroying tribes and traditional tributary states there as they did elsewhere. In Europe, they produced a way of life and a set of institutions that proved consistently more effective than any competitor at extracting power out of available resources and projecting it over space and through time at those who did not share these attitudes or institutions, whether fringe populations close to home or large nations far across the sea. Benjamin Franklin's *Autobiography*, the story of the first modern man in the first modern nation, remains an unsurpassed expression of the new European or Euro-American attitudes. It explained how the humble virtues of industry and frugality and the desire to "conquer all" personal "natural inclination, custom and company" allowed its author to accumulate wealth and power (Franklin, 66). The European conquest of the world was, in a sense, a spatial expression of the personal initiative and conquest exemplified in Franklin's life.

2

Revolution

Europeans conquered the world through the combined power of war, trade, and ideas. The most important idea was the supremacy of individual initiative, expressed eventually in the idea of individual rights and embodied in the liberal nation-state. War, trade, and ideas worked together in different ways, in different places, at different times. The role of military force and the ideas that justified and yet limited its use changed over the years, for example. Overall, however, Europeans developed military technology, skills, and dispositions that allowed them to seize much of the earth's surface and then hold it for a long period of time in the face of opposition. From the beginning of the conquest, a few Europeans questioned whether it was right to forcibly subject others. Over time, these questions were asked by more and more. The inquiry into the morality of empire was rooted in some of the same ideas that had originally motivated the great European going-out-over-the-world, principally the notion of individual initiative or self-determination or rights. Did not those who were enslaved or conquered by Europeans also have these rights? What had built European and then Euro-American empire would ultimately undermine it, even as Euro-American military technology and power remained unsurpassed. This chapter examines the military and moral revolutions that together help explain the rise and fall of Euro-American empire, as a groundwork for understanding resistance to and retreat from empire in the twentieth century.

The Military Revolution

All societies, tribal, tributary, or liberal, must extract wealth from the resources under their control, transform that wealth into coercive power, and project that power over space and through time. Projecting power over space through time means that a society controls a space and can exploit whatever is in it. It can make things happen in that space that would not happen otherwise. The extent, intensity, and duration of this control and exploitation depends on the sources of energy available to a society and the ideas that direct its use. If, for example, the way people think about the society and state they are part of encourages them to willingly submit to its laws and actively accept the demands of citizenship, then the state will more easily and more thoroughly mobilize and exploit the resources, both human and natural, that it controls. One reason for greater European power was that people proved more willing to give resources (their money or their labor) in exchange for rights and protection than for protection alone. The *levée en masse* that helped sweep republican France to victory following the revolution is an example of this. Regardless of the degree of human mobilization, however, human muscle fed by the products of photosynthesis will produce less energy than chemical or nuclear reactions. A society that relies on human muscle will have less energy at its disposal and less power to project over space through time than one that can harness not just the occasional draught animal but chemical and nuclear reactions. The more wealth a society extracts from its space, the more it can control and exploit that space; the more it controls and exploits it, the more wealth it can extract. Power produces plenty; plenty produces power. Europeans developed the most effective and efficient ways of exploiting resources the world had known and thus they had the means to conquer the world. Those who wanted to resist them had to adopt these means—ideas, technologies, institutions—or find others. (Throughout this discussion, I am improvising on ideas in Landers. Parry 1981, 19–21, explains the Spanish motivation for conquest in part with some similar ideas.)

Hunter-gatherers relied on the energy of human muscles to extract wealth from what nature provided. Nature's provision was the direct (plants) or indirect (animals) product of photosynthesis. Hunter-gatherers might get some additional energy from burning wood for warmth or to process food. They might fashion bows from branches and animal intestines or throwing weapons from tendons and stones. Such technology increased their power, but they were still essentially limited to what they could do with their own muscles. Using this limited energy source, they were able to extract little from the environment, perhaps no more than they invested in its exploitation. When returns dropped below this, they had to move on or perish. Their ability to exploit their environment was as limited as their ability to defend it. Agricultural societies added the energy of animals, wind, and water to human muscle. Exploiting these energy sources with harness, sail, and wheel, agricultural societies were able to extract more wealth from their environment than hunter-gatherers could. Some agricultural societies extracted significant wealth from their resources and increased it through trade. Others remained poor, especially in poor environments, or failed altogether when climate changed. With more energy at their disposal, agriculturalists were also likely to have better means to extend and defend the space under their control. Greater available energy would mean, for example, that they would be able to produce metal weapons and armor. Which metals they could produce depended on what technologies and ores were available.

Extracting wealth and extending and defending power required mobilizing human resources. Kinship ties formed social units, but beyond small bands it is difficult to see how such ties could be effective. To mobilize larger groups, thousands of people, something less restrictive than biological kinship was necessary. Common descent became fictive, therefore. Common descent "is less a strict biological rule than a convenient fiction for establishing social obligation." It is less a biological fact and more an idea. Some social entrepreneur, we suppose, found a way to take the individualistic worship of ancestors and use it to unify large numbers of people, perhaps by appealing to an ancient mythical ancestor. Once accepted, common descent could bind large numbers, giving such a social unit an advantage in war. Other societies would thus be compelled to follow suit or perish. Tribal societies were thus held together by certain religious ideas and beliefs. "If those beliefs change due to the introduction of a new religion, then the tribal form of organization can break down." This is what happened in Europe as Christianity spread, and it is what happened, often less thoroughly, as Europeans and Americans spread Christianity around the world (Fukuyama, 59, 61, 62–63; Woodberry).

As in other fields of human endeavor, in war, agrarian societies were dependent largely on human muscle power, supplemented by animals (horses, elephants, and dogs, for example, the first and last of these important in the Spanish conquests); some basic ballistic technologies, such as bows and catapults, fired from a distance; or shock technologies (cutting or bashing), such as swords and clubs, swung up close. Those who employed weapons up close developed armor for protection when possible; those using ballistic weapons relied on concealment, cover, and evasion for defense. Those with ballistic technologies could strike first, but up-close cutting and bashing tended to be more lethal and definitive. Horses were more mobile than men, but they were expensive to maintain, as were armored forces, because of the greater energy required to produce their armor. At or about the subsistence level, agrarian societies need just about everyone involved in agriculture in order to survive. This requirement limits labor specialization, including specialization in the use of coercive force. Professional soldiers were often scarce, as scarce as professional bandits. In the absence of specialization, coercive force reflected means and methods familiar in everyday life. For example, the tools of hunting tended to be the implements of war. This was the situation of many peoples that Europeans encountered in the western hemisphere. In South Asia, sufficient wealth existed to support some professional soldiers.

From these basic elements and characteristics, agrarian societies organized their military forces in different ways, depending on available resources and social structure. These forces consisted of some combination of shock and ballistic troops, heavy (armored) or light, mounted or on foot. The mix of troops was necessary because no one kind of force could reliably triumph over all others. Heavy cavalry or infantry could overcome light troops, but they were vulnerable to ballistic weapons and more mobile forces attacking their flanks or rear. Cavalry could not overcome disciplined troops formed and armed to meet their direct charge, as the Araucanians showed the Spanish (see chapter one). But such troops could be flanked and were themselves vulnerable to ballistic weapons. Centuries of warfare had developed tactics and weapons to exploit the advantages and disadvantage of each kind of force in a variety of circumstances and terrains. The Roman legion was virtually invincible in the field, but not in the forest, where it could not maneuver or effectively fight en masse and where, as a result, Arminius, leading German tribal forces, was able to destroy three legions in 9 CE. In addition, some military skills (using the longbow or a bow when mounted) were so difficult to master that doing so required their use to be part of a way of life, as was the case with the famous English yeoman and his bow or the Mongols and Plains Indians and their horses. Such ways of life and military systems depended on certain social and ecological conditions and thus were limited by these conditions, in turn limiting their military utility. Mongol cavalry re-quired vast grassy plains for forage, which did not exist in Europe. Mounted armored knights depended on socially validated conceptions of prestige and honor and a stratified society to support their expensive way of war. The an-cient Greek phalanx was an efficient way to use amateur soldiers but neces-sitated bonds of trust among its members, arguably compatible only with an egalitarian, communal political system. The Swiss produced successful infantry formations centuries later because Swiss life was communal and more egalitarian than others, a situation, like that of the Greek city-state, that did not exist everywhere. The result of these various limitations was that prior to the sixteenth century, at about the time the European conquest began, agrarian societies had not produced a "globally hegemonic system, a system capable of overcoming any opposition and spreading without limit through conquest or imitation" (Landers, 152, 136–37, 142).

If hunter-gatherer or agrarian populations were sparse enough in a given space, a powerful society could take control of that space and its nat-ural resources by overcoming mostly natural obstacles. Taking control of space when human populations were denser almost always meant overcom-ing human opposition. This entailed not only conquering human opponents but also controlling the space inhabited and organized by those just con-quered. If the space to be conquered had locations that were valuable, loca-tions of concentrated wealth (e.g., cities), these would be defended. In order to conquer such locations, the attacker would need to concentrate forces. Once these places were taken, the conqueror had to disperse his forces to control the entire space, since in agrarian societies wealth is ultimately as dispersed as agriculture is. To extend their power over space through time, then, agrarian societies had to both concentrate and disperse their forces. Concentration or dispersal varied depending on the character of the space to be conquered (Landers, 222). In India and South America, Europeans had to concentrate their forces and allies in order to conquer cities, then dis-perse them to control the conquered territories. In North America, the issue was more how to disperse forces to assert effective control, as there were fewer cities, Amerindian settlements were often movable, and most wealth (timber, animal furs, for example) could not be concentrated.

Given the energy resources available to agrarian societies, neither con-centrating nor dispersing forces was easy. Concentrated forces were difficult to supply. If they lived off the land, they quickly exhausted available supplies. They had to keep moving, but on foot and with pack trains or wagons, such forces moved slowly. Good, disciplined, and sufficiently fed heavy infantry might march twenty miles a day. Cavalry could cover two or three times that distance, but not if they were then to enter battle. Terrain and weather were significant factors (Landers, 220, 205). Thick forest or boggy land could slow troops to a crawl. Moving south from Canada early in the American Revolutionary War, a British army under General John Burgoyne managed only a few miles a day, its passage made more difficult by enemy harassment. Sieges of places of concentrated wealth often failed because the besiegers could not be supplied or exhausted the supplies available in the surrounding countryside, or in agrarian societies had to return home to bring in the harvest. Dispersing a concentrated force to control space eased the problems of living off the land but did not remove them. Hostile locals might hide what they had or even destroy it rather than let the invaders have it. In North America, much of the land was not developed and so might fail to support even small detachments. Transport of supplies was difficult through dense forest and over mountains. Troops tended to move by river and lake, as did their supplies. Controlling large forces was difficult because of the limited ability of commanders to communicate. The need to disperse forces aggravated this problem. Lack of effective communications between different parts of North America often undid sound strategic planning. Concentrating dispersed forces on a strategic objective often proved impossible (consider Anderson, 388, 409–10).

One way to overcome some of the problems of dispersing forces was to build forts. Fortifications were a way of depositing the collected wealth, and thus power (food, weapons, men), of a conqueror in the space of the conquered. They were the mirror, if more rustic, image of the urban concentrations of wealth that conquerors had to take control of. The Amerindians, having only augmented human and animal muscle power, could not reduce prepared fortifications. They had to starve out the defenders, but such effort was costly to the attackers, who had to attend constantly to their own provisioning. Because their societies had a limited division of labor, Amerindian warriors could not be full-time soldiers. If the defenders were sufficiently provisioned or regularly supplied or could communicate to colleagues their need for reinforcements and provisions to withstand the Amerindian siege, the defenders could usually outlast the besiegers. This explains the Spanish success at Cuzco (see chapter one). It also explains why during Pontiac's

Rebellion the three most important English forts—Niagara, Detroit, and Pittsburgh—did not fall and the rebellion failed in its immediate objectives. Fortified enclaves gave Europeans a foothold in Asia (Childs, 39). It was from these that the British conquered India.

The difficulties in concentrating and dispersing forces, and thus in conquering and controlling space, help explain the limits of agrarian empires. Although these empires could sometimes grow quite large, as the Roman and Mongol cases prove, they eventually reached limits, and the intensity and duration of their control varied. The Mongols, whose large unified empire lasted only about 160 years, tended to be absorbed into the societies they conquered, indicating the limited intensity of their control. Rome endured significantly longer because it more thoroughly penetrated the areas it controlled. It did this through trade, and by attending to issues of communication and transport (the famous Roman roads), but also by deploying an idea. The Romans inculcated the idea of *romanitas* or Roman-ness among those they conquered, granting many citizenship. (The French used similar means in their imperial endeavors in the nineteenth and twentieth centuries, establishing monetary unions in Africa and offering Frenchness as a universal way of being human.) The Romans also incorporated the gods of the conquered into Roman religion. (French Catholicism sometimes became syncretic in Africa.) The Roman empire became valuable to those who were made part of it, a pre-liberal example of how protection and "rights" in exchange for taxes was a more effective extraction bargain than just protection alone.

Because coercive force was a costly way to maintain conquest and control, trade and ideas became essential parts of intense and enduring empire. Yet even the Roman empire had its limits. Every empire has frontiers or marches, areas where its control fades. In these areas, warfare is often "chronic," as opposed to warfare in areas of concentrated wealth and concentrated forces where it is "acute" (Landers, 222). Acute warfare consists of large organized forces engaged in set-piece or sometimes even decisive battles for control of the cities where wealth is concentrated. Such battles determine political control because places of concentrated wealth tend also to be places of concentrated politico-religious authority. The capital city— Paris or Berlin—was the target of European acute warfare. Chronic warfare consists of raiding, ambushing, "skulking," destroying crops and settlements and their inhabitants. It takes place over lengthy periods of time, often in hopes of wearing down either resistance to conquest or the will to conquer. This is the kind of warfare that developed between the Spanish and the Araucanians in South America and between Europeans and the Amerindians of North America. Chronic warfare occurs not just at the limits of empire, as the ability to extend power over space and through time fades. It may be the only way to control space with coercive force when the inhabitants have few fixed assets of any value, such as the Plains Amerindians or some revolutionaries in the twentieth century, who developed their own version of chronic warfare, which they called protracted war (see chapter four), a version of which we now call terrorism. The less concentrated wealth a people has to defend, the more able and likely they are to engage in chronic warfare. In these cases as well, trade and ideas, especially the former, may be as important as coercive force for conquest and control. Trade is voluntary, thus easier and less energy consuming than coercion, but it can change a way of life even more thoroughly than force can.

The difficulties of conquest and control might be prohibitively expensive compared with what might be gained by control alone, although it is doubtful that such calculations were made precisely, if at all. Calculations of some sort seem to have occurred, however, since superior powers did devise means of controlling people without conquering them. They could, for example, rest with making a people and their space dependent on the superior power by demanding payments or by making them. A superior power could coerce an inferior into paying tribute, rather than itself imposing the sort of intensive administrative control necessary for extracting resources (e.g., taxes). The tribute was payment for protection, either from the violence of the superior power demanding it or from the violence of other superior powers. While Rome extracted resources directly from the peoples it conquered, stateless conquerors such as the Mongols or Iroquois were often capable only of compelling tribute. They lacked the bureaucratic apparatus to extract revenue, although in some cases conquerors (the Mongols in China, the British in India) could take over already existing direct systems of revenue extraction. The other arrangement of dependence involved the reverse of tribute, the imperial power paying those on its perimeter to serve as mercenaries to fight other frontier peoples (often done with the Amerindians in the western hemisphere, as we have seen) or to serve as a buffer between the empire and another imperial power. This was the British method with the tribes on the northwest frontier of India in the nineteenth and early twentieth centuries.

These basic patterns of agrarian warfare and empire remained in place unchanged for centuries until the energy that propelled them changed. That occurred with the adoption of gunpowder weapons. This was an epochal development, "the first time that muscle power had been supplanted by chemical energy as the primary power source in a major area of human activity" (Landers, 8). Used in China since the seventh or eighth centuries, gunpowder reached Europe in the late thirteenth century. Cannons appeared in the early fourteenth century, handguns shortly after. By the early sixteenth century, the matchlock musket was in use, along with iron cannon. These gunpowder weapons replaced earlier ballistic weapons (bows and catapults), and they revolutionized warfare. Massed firepower could now overwhelm cavalry, which began its descent to the supporting role of scouting, foraging, and protecting the flanks of massed infantry.

One needed disciplined and trained troops to mass firepower effectively, however, especially since to make their fire effective, musket-bearing infantry needed to fire in unison (their guns were too inaccurate to aim individually) then retire to reload behind another line of musket infantry that stepped forward prepared to fire. This line then retired to reload as the line behind them, already loaded, stepped forward. Initially, given the difficulty of loading early muskets, several lines were required to keep up a continuous fire. As weapons improved, the number of lines decreased. Always, however, drill, discipline and organization were necessary to keep up orderly movement among lines of infantry and thus an effective rate of fire. Anyone could learn this drill rather quickly, but it had to be practiced. A more developed and differentiated rank structure to control the movement of infantry lines and to drill and train soldiers to carry out their coordinated tasks was also necessary. The advent of infantry firepower thus tended to lead to professional or full-time hierarchically organized armies dominated by infantry and artillery. Because the drill of loading a musket and moving with it could be broken into a system of steps that anyone could learn with practice, warfare lost its connection to any particular way of life, whether the English yeomen's or the nomadic horsemen's. It thus also lost the limitation imposed by relying on a way of life. Infantry-based firepower warfare could become a universal way of fighting. Other kinds of specialized troops tended to disappear from the battlefield, as infantry with muskets, especially tipped with a bayonet that did not hinder firing, proved versatile. As the infantry firepower system spread, what tended to determine the outcome of battles was the amount of firepower and hence the number of men engaged in the battle. Even as generalship, experience, morale, terrain, and chance remained important and occasionally decisive, the number of soldiers engaged increased in importance as a determining factor. Armies in Europe grew in size (Childs; Black 2005; Landers, 171).

Gunpowder also affected naval warfare. Artillery on ships meant that they no longer had to ram or pull alongside in order to damage enemy vessels. Sails could thus replace oars on fighting ships, since oars had been preferred for the maneuverability and reliability ramming required. Wind power in turn increased cruising range, as sailing ships had fewer crew members than and a different shape and construction from rowed ships. Fewer crew members meant smaller quantities of food and water for cruises; the different shape and construction made it possible to accommodate the necessary supplies. As their size and construction changed, the largest sailing warships eventually developed a tiered array of artillery. With their increased firepower and cruising range, European ships could travel thousands of miles and defeat the fleets they then encountered (Landers, 189–90, 191–92; Black 2005, 45). This ability gave the Portuguese their advantage in the Indian Ocean. Naval power allowed the Portuguese to extract or extort plenty. The Dutch, French, and British followed suit, and with greater resources first extracted at home, extended their control over the sea.

As armies and navies grew in size, they imposed increasing financial burdens on the states that employed them. Large portions of state expenditure were given over to military establishments. At one point in the eighteenth century, Russia spent 60 percent of its revenue on its military in peacetime and 95 percent in wartime. At about the same time, Britain was spending about 75 percent of its revenue on the military during wartime; France, about the same (Childs, 33). The burdens became so great that some states faced bankruptcy. Governments used various means to meet the financial demands of warfare. They borrowed money. Some "farmed" tax collection, turning it and the money raised over to individuals in return for a payment. Beginning at the time of the Glorious Revolution (1689), and continuing during the Second Hundred Years' War with France that followed, Britain developed a fiscal system that proved better at financing war than that of any other European state. Because wars were ruinously expensive, the state that could most quickly recover financially from the last one was in a position to start the next one before its adversaries. This gave Britain the advantage of the initiative.

The British had developed an excise or internal tax system that was intrusive, professional, competent, skilled, transparent, and honest, at least by the standards of the day. "The excise employed a complex system of bookkeeping and measuring both to tax such commodities as beer, hops, malt, spirits, tea, coffee, leather, salt, soap, candles and wire and to ensure the probity of its employees." This system, along with higher tax rates, increased British tax revenue sixfold in the hundred years from the mid-seventeenth to the mid-eighteenth century. This increase did not cover the rising expenses of the state and its warmaking, but it did allow the British government to borrow the rest in an efficient and sustainable way. Pledging the receipts from a particular tax to pay interest on a specific debt, such as that for navy ordinance, funded the debt, making it a long-term obligation guaranteed by a specific tax. The guarantee made it a safe or safer investment. Those who lent money knew that a specific tax receipt would pay them the interest on the money they had lent the government. The safety of the debt encouraged more lending, even as the total debt mounted. The financial system also bound the wealthy to the state, giving it added stability. Finally, this system was part of the Treasury, which oversaw both collection and expenditure and made Britain "the first major European state to keep full accounts of total government revenue and expenditure." This uniquely powerful financial system supported Britain's navy and army. It was the sinew of British power, and that power was a key part of building the British empire (Brewer 1993, 59, 58, 60; Brewer 1988, 114–20).

The European infantry system brought about by the development of gunpowder weapons proved capable of defeating any other military system and so became universal in Europe. Sufficient drill and placement in the proper military structure could turn any unskilled individual into a useful soldier. With the assistance of local allies, including indigenous unskilled recruits, and adaptations to local circumstances, the European infantry system proved similarly capable outside of Europe. It defeated the various powers in India. It was in this sense a hegemonic military system (Landers, 174, 195; Childs, 39; Black 2005, 44, 45, 46). With the support of powerful oceanic navies, the military means to extend European control were increasingly available as the eighteenth and nineteenth centuries progressed. The French subdued Corsica in 1769 with a substantial force sustained from France that fought, absorbed losses, but continued to attack, building roads that extended the reach of military and ultimately French civil power (Black 2005, 53). In the years to come, the French would repeat this effort across the Mediterranean in Algeria and eventually in Southeast Asia.

The hegemonic European military system relied on the development of a fiscal-military state to finance it. Not every European country had such a system, or at least a system like Britain's, but the tendency was to move in that direction as the evidence of the effectiveness of Britain's system accumulated. Some proof of the appeal of the system is that as part of a government recently freed from British imperial domination, Alexander Hamilton, in charge of the Treasury Department, proposed this system for the United States in George Washington's first administration. He deemed it essential for national greatness. Thus, the fiscal system also became hegemonic. It not only allowed the Europeans to project their power and influence abroad; it also allowed them to consolidate power at home. It centralized and strengthened domestic government. All subjects paid tax and became increasingly subject to the control and surveillance of the increasingly powerful government. In addition to augmenting the power of government, the fiscal-military revolution also produced political, economic, and social changes. It created a financial class or interest, people who owned part of the public debt and who, with their finances thus secured, could gain advantages in private money markets. As the power of government increased, especially in finance and the economy, it became an object of lobbying by special interests (Brewer 1988, 121–22, 250–51). By bringing professional military forces and standing armies to the fore, it contributed to the division and specialization of labor in society as a whole. Professional standing armies in time created the problem of civil-military relations, of establishing a process through which civilians could control the powerful militaries they had created. This remained a problem for the Euro-American state into the twentieth century (see chapter four; Feaver). The military revolution, then, entailed a fiscal revolution and, in building the power of the state, was part of a political and even social revolution.

This fiscal-military revolution took place over several hundred years, roughly 1500 to 1800. It began as the Spanish were setting out on their conquest of South America and continued through the British conquest of

India. Can something with such an extended timeline be called a revolution? If we think of a revolution as a single cataclysmic event, then it would be wrong to call the development in Europe of a hegemonic system of warfare a revolution. It was, rather, a set of interconnected developments set in motion by the adoption of firearms in the circumstances prevailing in early modern Europe. Famously, these circumstances included almost continuous Europe-wide warfare from the late fifteenth century through the middle of the seventeenth, followed by the Second Hundred Years' War (1688–1815), which included the first global war, the Seven Years' War (1756–63). Military change led or contributed to political, economic, and social change, which in turn allowed other military changes, which in their turn affected economics, politics, and society. To call this set of changes a "revolution" requires seeing the term in its sense of a continuous circular movement, perhaps imagining a snowball rolling down a hill growing in size. Or we might conceive of the circular movement as a spiraling series of events, the sum greater somehow than the mere addition of its parts, whose outcome could not have been predicted from the analysis of the momentum of any of those individual parts.

An illustration of the complex character of the military revolution understood as an economic, political, and social event is the effect of the European conquest on the Industrial Revolution and the Industrial Revolution on the second phase of European conquest in the nineteenth century. The first phase of conquest (roughly 1500–1800) occurred when the socioeconomic basis of European life was not much different from the way of life of those the Europeans conquered. Agrarian people conquered agrarian people. This first conquest made available to the European economy vast tracts of land and large numbers of laborers, principally in the western hemisphere. As the cost of transportation declined in the nineteenth century, the distance of these resources from European markets in effect declined as well, and their influence on these markets increased. As this occurred, the cost of both food and land declined in Europe, as the supply of both in the now global European economy increased. This meant in turn that "industrial growth could continue for longer, without being choked off by rising input costs." In addition, lower transport costs and larger foreign markets meant that European countries could produce more without this increased supply reducing prices. The overall effect was "that a given domestic impulse (in this case, technological change) propelled the British economy much farther than would otherwise have been the case" (Findlay and O'Rourke, 342–43).

For a variety of reasons (political, demographic, geographic), Great Britain was best placed, as the earliest and most complete industrializer in Europe, to take advantage of the first phase of conquest. Nevertheless, all industrializing European countries benefited; so too would the United States. If the extent of foreign markets was a boost to industrialization, then "it seems reasonable to conclude that British military successes overseas [which gave them those foreign markets] played an important role in explaining why Britain, rather than France, was so successful and precocious an industrializer" (Findlay and O'Rourke, 352). Power helped produce plenty.

Plenty powered the second phase of the European conquest during the long nineteenth century, which ended in 1914. Critical for the second phase was the move from organic to mineral sources of energy. Coal had been in use, of course, for a long time before 1800, but the development of the steam engine allowed the exploitation of its greater density of energy compared to wood, marking a definitive break with the limitations of human and animal muscle energy. "By 1800 England consumed a volume of coal with an energy content equivalent to woodlands covering 50–100 per cent of the country's surface area and thereby broke through the fundamental 'hard' limit of the organic economy." One estimate is that in the late eighteenth century Europeans had available to them from animals, wind, water, and wood about twenty times the energy of unaided human muscle. In industrial economies, humans have available several hundred times the energy of unaided human muscle (Landers, 50, 122; Findlay and O'Rourke, 320–21). Steam revolutionized navigation, lowering the costs of transportation, especially combined with the construction of canals, particularly at Suez and Panama. In doing so, it increased the ability of Europeans to project their commercial and military power abroad. Steam-powered navigation freed commercial and war ships from the unreliable wind and allowed them to navigate the rivers of Africa and Asia, extending and deepening the European penetration of those continents. On land, steam-powered railroads had a similar effect on commerce and on warfare, as they increased both the mobility of armies and the ability to supply them (Headrick, 177–217; Findlay and O'Rourke, 378–87). Coal (later oil) and steam turned into what we might call the hegemonic sources of energy to complement the already hegemonic European infantry and financial systems.

The growing European military hegemony in the nineteenth century did not mean that the Europeans were always victorious. They lost battles, even if they eventually prevailed in acute warfare. A tribal charge of the sort the British defeated at Culloden (1746) overwhelmed British forces when Zulus mounted it against them at Isandlwana (1879). Other European defeats included those suffered by the Italians at the hands of the Ethiopians at Dogali (1887) and Adwa (1896); the French by the Chinese at the battle of Bang Bo (1885); and the Americans by the Sioux, Cheyenne, and Arapaho at Little Bighorn (1876). Euro-American forces had to overcome serious resistance. But "precisely because non-Western societies were not decrepit, primitive, underdeveloped or weak, the Western success in conquering large areas was a formidable military achievement" (Black 2002, 5; Black 2005, 43). The Industrial Revolution not only increased Euro-American resources and power projection, but it also helped produce an array of increasingly powerful weapons as technological innovation transformed firepower. In the nineteenth century, Euro-American power—British, French, Russian, and American—prevailed, despite setbacks and continuing resistance, as trade, war, and ideas continued to work together. As British arms took control of India, the efficiencies of industrialized British manufacture and the decreasing costs of transportation created a market for finished British textiles in India, reversing, as previously noted, the flow of trade that had originally brought finished Indian cotton textiles to Britain.

The transforming power of technology is so impressive that it has led some to argue that a series of discrete military technological revolutions have occurred in European history, stretching from the fourteenth through the twentieth centuries. As this view gained a hold in the American military bureaucracy in the 1990s, the term "revolution in military affairs" (RMA) came to mean "the application of new technologies into a significant number of military systems combin[ing] with innovative operational concepts and organizational adaptation in a way that fundamentally alters the character and conduct of conflict" (Krepinevich, 30) and that gives an advantage to the forces transformed by the RMA. Sifting the facts of history with the filter of this definition led its author to identify ten RMAs: infantry; artillery; sail and shot; fortress; gunpowder; Napoleonic; land warfare; naval; mechanization, aviation, information; and nuclear. This analysis, carried out in the aftermath of the First Gulf War (1990–91), then raised the question whether an eleventh revolution was occurring as information technology changed how militaries fought. In the Gulf War, U.S. forces had combined precision-strike weapons and surveillance technology to devastating effect. Had information technology created another RMA?

All aspects of the RMA story, historical as well as contemporary, have occasioned debate and controversy (e.g., Rogers; Biddle 2004; Biddle 2005–6). That debate helps explain the development of European warfare, but it is less important for understanding Euro-American empire. From the 500-year perspective of this empire, continuities stand out. "The European tactical system of 1914 was nonetheless the recognizable lineal descendant of the musket and sabre system of 1714" (Landers, 158). The trench system used by the Vietminh to besiege and defeat the French at Dien Bien Phu in 1954 was almost unchanged from the trench system the French had used in 1757 to besiege and defeat British forces at Fort William Henry. But whether these continuities outweigh the changes that occurred over those 500 years is not critical to understanding the rise of European empire. The crux there is the change that gunpowder first wrought and its connection to the rise of the fiscal-military state. It was this change in warfare and the revolving interrelated set of changes in government, politics, economics, and warfare it set in motion that built the states that gained imperial power (Tilly). Moreover, much of imperial warfare was not acute warfare, where revolutions are arguably evident and important, but chronic warfare, where they are not.

In chronic warfare, revolutions seem not to appear at all. When Caesar fought the Gauls, he used the same tactics the Americans would later use against the Amerindians in the seventeenth century and after, the same the British would use against tribes in the northwest territories of India in the nineteenth. Against those who did not stand and fight, force was applied to what could not move or protect itself: settlements, food, noncombatants. This made chronic warfare brutal but not necessarily more brutal than acute warfare (Black 2005, 51). If not in brutality, the two kinds of warfare did differ in other ways. First, acute warfare, at least as Europeans experienced it after the gunpowder revolution, was primarily a contest between professional disciplined forces. Their conduct was not always exemplary, but they were subject to better control than the irregular forces involved in chronic warfare. Second, chronic warfare was virtually indistinguishable from the destruction of civilians and their property, whereas acute warfare aimed primarily and most often at the destruction of military forces. Third, acute warfare was fought to control valuable territory or for national survival. Chronic warfare typically occurred in less-valuable space, on frontiers or in marginal areas, often with people considered incorrigibly barbaric and of little utility to the imperial project. Finally, and related to the third point, acute warfare was fierce but limited temporally. One could distinguish such war from peace; harsh methods were temporary and necessary to restore peace or ensure survival. Chronic war seemed to have no temporal end and might seem to have no moral end or purpose either, therefore. Given these differences, the justification for chronic warfare was always more difficult than for acute warfare. This difficulty would grow over time, making chronic warfare increasingly hard to wage.

The Moral Revolution

Empire—extending power over space through time—almost always meant extending power over human beings. For most of human history, the only issue about power over human beings was how it was to be acquired and retained, not whether it was right to have it. The Vikings who conquered areas of Eastern Europe and sold the inhabitants to the Arabs do not seem to have concerned themselves with questions of right. By the time the European conquest began, this disinterest was no longer the case. As Thomas Jefferson noted, although not explicitly regarding the issue of empire, Christianity had changed things. The greatness of ancient philosophy, according to Jefferson, was its understanding of what we owe ourselves; the greatness of Jesus was his understanding of what we owe others (Jefferson, 1124–25, 1431). By raising the issue of the status of others and thus whether it was right to hold power over them, Christianity raised the question of whether acquiring and retaining empire was right. Of course, Christianity had its own universal, even imperial, claims. It was not a religion restricted to one place or one nation. It aimed at power over all human beings, and an unprecedented power. It sought not just outward conformity to a law but an inward transformation or reorientation of life. It would be more accurate to say, then, that Christianity raised the question of how power over humans should be acquired and retained. According to the New Testament, conversion was to be by example and persuasion, not force of arms. Converts were to come to Christ willingly, not through coercion, and for their own good, not for the benefit of the converter, which was why persuasion would work.

By the time the European conquest began, Christianity had long since become political (unlike Judaism and Islam, its cousins, which were political in their origins), and politics is unavoidably coercive. Christianity, therefore, had made an uneasy peace with coercion. (In the case of the conquistadores, it seems to have been a happy marriage.) Despite its political character, and its use of coercion against heretics and others, the Church did in various ways also try to limit the use of violence in human affairs. Not only did the political character of the Church complicate this effort; the reasonings of its theologians and canon lawyers did as well. Christ taught that we must love our neighbors, but an emperor might ask, who is my neighbor? There are different sorts of neighbors—some threatening, some not; some civilized, some not; some Christian, some not—and being Christian and being civilized were not always taken to be synonymous. If all must be loved, must all be treated the same? And how is one to judge who is a Christian? One of the most important issues concerned what made all humans brothers in Christ. Was it grace or natural law? If God's law, natural law, was decisive, a claim most fully compatible with the belief that man's reason had survived the fall, then all men had claims that all others were bound in some measure to respect. By contrast, if grace, God's gift, is decisive, then the heathen, those who had not received it, might not have claims that those who had received grace need respect. If all rights, including the right to hold property, came through God's grace, as mediated by his anointed sovereign deputies on earth (kings or popes), could the heathen have any right to property (Pagden, 75, 95)? And if they had no right to property, then driving them from the land could not be wrong. (A later secular version of this argument held that property was only that with which a man had mixed his labor. If land were left undeveloped, it could not be anyone's property and thus taking it could not be wrong.) Could those who had left land undeveloped be coerced, if not into Christianity then at least into being civilized? Could they be ruled against their will for their own good?

From the Middle Ages into the early modern period, when the European conquest began, considering such questions had led to the development of principles of restraint, not universally acknowledged, often unobserved, for the application of coercive force to others. Those most likely to benefit from restraint were neighbors considered civilized and Christian—and in the case of subjects, those considered loyal. Such principles were grounded not only in theology but in prudence as well. Shakespeare has Henry V say to his army as they try to conquer France:

> We give express charge, that in our marches through the
> country, there be nothing compelled from the
> villages, nothing taken but paid for, none of the
> French upbraided or abused in disdainful language;
> for when lenity and cruelty play for a kingdom, the
> gentler gamester is the soonest winner.

Sometimes it was useful as well as right to treat one's neighbors well. But it could also be useful, on occasion, to treat them ill. Exemplary atrocities could make conquest easier. The Mongols supposedly burned and pillaged a town after raping, torturing, and murdering the inhabitants, letting a few escape to spread the word so that neighboring towns would surrender without a fight. Assuming in their own case the justice of their conquest, Europeans wondered if the atrocity that led to surrender, and thus reduced harm to other noncombatants, might be just (Parker, 49–50).

If moral reasoning had an effect on European imperialism, it was largely to condone the use of force against non-Christians or the uncivilized, such as the indigenous peoples of the Americas (the uncivilized included the Irish). Some Spanish churchmen objected to the dispossession and coerced labor of the Amerindians while others saw the spread of Spanish empire as an opportunity to spread the gospel, and eternal salvation as more important than earthly happiness. The British settlers in North America spent more time dispossessing the natives than trying to convert them. French missionaries had an easier time mitigating brutality and focused on converting the Amerindians, but they had an easier task since the French did not want to settle the land as much as harvest the skins of the animals that roamed it, and they needed the Amerindians as harvesters and allies against the British. On the plantations of the new world, African slaves were objects of conversion, but many were denied even that acknowledgment of their humanity for fear of the consequences. They were property too valuable in the production of wealth from sugar, and later cotton, to be tampered with. (In the east, except at sea, the Europeans only gradually gained the power to compel; questions of right rose gradually as well, therefore.)

These attitudes toward empire and those subject to it began to change in a politically significant way toward the end of the eighteenth century, as Jefferson's remarks about Christianity and duty to others indicate. The change consisted not in the extension of the older notions of restraint to those not previously benefiting from them but in the development of a new understanding of what was owed to others. That new understanding was the view that the most noble expression of human being was "a tender sentimental feeling of our own and other's [sic] misfortunes" (quoted in Crane, 206). Reacting against the views of the Puritans and Thomas Hobbes that men were naturally selfish, a group of divines and philosophers in the late seventeenth and early eighteenth century began insisting that men were endowed with social passions, chief among them benevolence, or an awareness of and regard for others. The divines held up before their congregations and readers as a model of Christian charity "the tenderhearted Christian, pitying before he relieves." In first feeling and then seeking to relieve the pain of others, Christians would be "actualizing the beneficent designs of God for man and . . . realizing the aim of religion to perfect human nature" (Crane, 217, 211). God was benevolent and loving toward his creatures, and all men should strive to imitate the divine. Among philosophers the most prominent early exponent of benevolence was Francis Hutcheson. Trained as a minister, Hutcheson devoted his life to moral philosophy. His publications (e.g., *An Inquiry into the Original of Our Ideas of Beauty and Virtue* [1726]) were widely influential in Britain and the United States. According to him, by God's design humans were naturally disposed to have concern for others and to take pleasure in helping them, which was the basis for their tendency to do so.

Through preaching, literature, and education (Hutcheson was a professor of ethics at the University of Glasgow; Adam Smith was one of his students), the notion that humans were and should be benevolent toward others gained adherents as the eighteenth century progressed. The first political expression of the emphasis on benevolence was the movement to stop the slave trade, which achieved success when Parliament passed an act prohibiting the trade in 1807. Hutcheson himself had pointed to the effect of his psychology of benevolence on the question of the rightness of slavery: "Must not all the sentiments of compassion and humanity, as well as reflection on the general interests of mankind, dissuade from such usage of captives [i.e., enslavement], even tho' it could be vindicated by some plea of external right?" (quoted in Fiering, 208).

Acknowledging rights of conquest (external right), if only because of their validation by custom, Hutcheson held up the claims of both sentiment and interest against slavery. Powered by such ideas, the effort to abolish the slave trade was perhaps the first time in human history that people had organized to address not their own suffering but the suffering of others, especially "others" who were remote and as different from those seeking to help them as middle-class Britons were from the slaves. Not only were the slaves remote, but relieving their suffering was contrary to the material interests of the British and their empire (Davis, 231–32).

The rise of benevolence and humanitarianism was a moral revolution (Crane, 206, 222; Fiering, 212). As one analyst has written, "The main innovation in ethics and psychology that allowed unqualified humanitarianism to flower was the discrediting of rational justifications for inhumanity by opposing to them the *divine authority* of natural and instinctive compassionate feeling" (Fiering, 208, emphasis in original). Hutcheson, for example, did not deny that there might be some plea of external right to justify slavery. Traditionally, he noted, captives in war could be enslaved. Despite this, slavery should be held illegitimate because it was counter to the compassionate feelings of men, which were ultimately an imitation of the compassionate feelings of God. Of great importance in the triumph of this view was evangelical Protestantism, which came to emphasize the emotional response to the call of God and in doing so reinforced the divine authority of human passions. Many adherents of this kind of Christianity came to believe that reform of the human condition was necessary to fulfill the providential design of history, in particular, to prepare the world for the second coming of Jesus Christ. This gave divinely validated human passions a cosmic significance. The evangelicals felt strongly that stopping the slave trade was part of God's plan and their Christian duty. Even many secular thinkers, such as Thomas Jefferson, came to hold the view that men by nature had an irresistible impulse "to feel and succor the . . . distresses of" others (Jefferson, 1337, 901–2; Fiering, 195).

Historically, irresistible compassion was the foundation of the humanitarianism that first found political expression in the movement to abolish the slave trade. Yet, in retrospect at least, humanitarianism seems paradoxical. If its principles were true, it should have been unnecessary. If it is true that humans have an irresistible impulse to feel and relieve the suffering of others, why did slavery exist in the first place? One might argue that the existence of slavery and other forms of cruelty shows that humanitarianism has no foundation in nature—nature being understood as that which universally tends to happen. Jefferson denied this and argued that instances of humans resisting compassion and acting cruelly or asocially were exceptions (Jefferson, 1337–38). But surely the course of human events suggests that cruelty is at least as common as kindness. On what basis do we select kindness, therefore, as natural? Christians could avoid this difficulty in the first instance by appealing to God's benevolence, rather than natural impulses, as the justification for their own compassion. They could explain brutality and cruelty as the stance of those who had not yet received God's grace (all the more reason to press forward with world evangelization) or as examples of spiritual weakness.

Christianity provided an apparently nonparadoxical foundation for humanitarianism. As Jefferson wrote, Christianity "went far beyond both [Judaism and ancient philosophy] in inculcating universal philanthropy, not only to kindred and friends, to neighbors and countrymen, but to all mankind, gathering all into one family, under the bonds of love, charity, peace, common wants and common aids" (Jefferson, 1125). Christianity, however, had always done this, yet humanitarianism was a phenomenon of the late eighteenth century and after. Christianity alone, therefore, cannot explain the rise of humanitarianism. Those who have excavated its foundations point to specific developments that combined with evangelical, sentimental Christianity to produce humanitarianism: modern science, the Enlightenment, and industrial capitalism (Barnett; Parmelee, 356; Porter, 200; Skinner and Lester, 733; Bender; Crane, 210, 221; Fiering, 198, 203, 209). For example, if one wants to champion liberty and limited government (against, for example, the Puritans and Hobbes), it is useful to argue that humans have benevolent, social passions that order life and society without requiring the heavy hand of government. This explains the connection between humanitarianism and laissez-faire capitalism (the connection between Hutcheson and Smith) and makes the former a good companion to the unbridled initiative characteristic of the European approach to the world.

It is the connection to freedom, or a particular conception of freedom, that above all indicates that humanitarianism is of modern and not just Christian inspiration. Traditionally, Christianity aimed to relieve human suffering through charity. Modern science aimed to relieve human suffering by giving human beings the power to change the world (cure disease, end famine, etc.). Manipulating nature in this way implied human separation or freedom from nature, which was, after all, according to modern science, simply matter in motion and as such indifferent to human concerns. In this understanding, reason came to be thought of not as the dialectical uncovering of the natural structure and purpose of the world but as merely the instrumental, largely calculating, skill necessary to arrange pliable matter into configurations deemed useful insofar as they relieved man's estate or satisfied his desires. By turning attention from Roman Catholic doctrine, which was Hellenized, toward the Bible, which was not, the Reformation contributed to this demotion of reason by helping to free western thought from the conviction that reason was the most important human attribute. In particular, this prepared the way for the humanitarian emphasis on the emotions. If one thinks, as science does, that reality is matter in motion, then one will tend to emphasize what moves humans (their emotions or passions), rather than their reason. Having done that, it was logical to see the immediate, instinctive response as superior to or more trustworthy than the deliberated reasoned outcome (Fiering, 207–8). As Jefferson put it, a ploughman, with his uncorrupted moral sense, was a more reliable judge in moral matters than a professor, since the latter was likely to be led astray by "artificial rules" (Jefferson, 901). (The disparagement of deliberation in ethics was the counterpart of the disparagement of dialectic in metaphysics.) The rise to prominence of benevolence and humanitarianism was not, then, only the result of the musings of some latitudinarian divines and fellow-traveling philosophers but the expression of a revolution in thinking about human psychology and the world more generally. In this regard, as one perceptive historian reminds us, "the discovery of the benevolent feelings seems to have preceded and forced the change in the understanding of God's will" (Fiering, 208). The result of this revolution was a focus on changing the world to relieve human suffering, the articulation of an understanding of science, ethics, and politics compatible with this ambition, and an unprecedented valuation of the passions as the best guides for its realization. (For a more detailed account of this revolution, consider Tucker 2014, esp. 16–41.)

The roots of humanitarianism in the scientific revolution and the Reformation explain the growth of this idea into an influential enduring force in modern life and its connection to other modern phenomena such as industrialization, technology, and capitalism. In this sense, humanitarianism was another aspect of the emphasis on human initiative that was central to Euro-American imperialism. It helps explain the restless, far-reaching character of humanitarianism. After ending the slave trade, humanitarians turned to the issue of slavery itself. After slavery was abolished in the British empire (1833), humanitarians took up the cause of the Aborigines or of the treatment of native peoples in that empire (Porter, 207). Throughout this period, and for the remainder of the empire's existence, the humanitarian impulse led Britons to question more and more the justice of their global rule. Although the humanitarian movement originated in Britain and was early on a powerful force in America, and while its heart beat strongest perhaps in the Anglo-American world, it spread beyond it. In the twentieth century, especially after World War II, humanitarianism became a worldwide movement. For example, this movement is now focused on promoting the new "norm" of the so-called responsibility to protect, which is held to supersede the sovereign power of states (G. Evans).

A powerful force in modern life, humanitarianism did not have a simple effect on imperialism. For example, representative government allowed humanitarianism to affect imperial politics. Humanitarian voters shaped imperial government policy. Yet representative government also meant that settlers in the empire could resist the efforts of the humanitarians back home through the self-rule the settlers denied to the indigenous. Furthermore, some humanitarians were disappointed with the benefits of the abolition and aboriginal protection movements, which led to a reassessment of the capacities of those subject to imperial rule and thus a reassessment of the critique of empire itself. Staunch liberals like John Stuart Mill argued that the right of self-determination might be ignored if done for the good of those whose right was ignored. At the same time, the duty to spread Christianity remained a justification for empire. Thus, the notion of empire as a trust became part of the humanitarian understanding of empire, even though it justified imperial rule, if not its brutal exercise.

By the late nineteenth century, as views of the indigenous became more favorable, humanitarianism led to a new critique of empire. But even as this critique became accepted, humanitarianism changed from a passion or feeling into a habit. The passion weakened as the original humanitarian impulse faded and as evangelical Christianity became a less powerful movement and one less focused on bringing about the millennium through reform (Fiering, 213; Porter, 214; Barnett). The humanitarian impulse became a reflex, often a hollow or contradictory one. Less willing to claim divine sanction for their humane impulses, humanitarians began to talk of imposing human-created "norms" on other humans, a different kind of conquest perhaps but still a conquest. Behind the caring face of humanitarianism is the rational technologized power that conquered the world. Humanitarianism became institutionalized, bureaucratized, an ally of governments, although uneasy about the alliance. Humanitarians attended both the Berlin conference in 1884 that divided up Africa among the imperial powers and the Brussels anti-slave-trade conference of 1890. From a movement, humanitarianism changed into a lobby, part of the technocratic governmental process (Porter, 216–17). It gave up efforts to transform indigenous society, although arguably this urge returned in the Bush administration's thinking about Iraq. Throughout its history, however, the moral revolution of humanitarianism called into question the forced subordination of others. In the 1950s, "a metropolitan humanitarian constituency" had come to reject empire, advocating "anti-colonial and liberation movements" (Skinner and Lester, 739). This constituency became an ally of indigenous people seeking to end empire.

A historical irony of the twentieth century is that as Europeans became less inclined to use violence against others, they became more inclined to use violence among themselves. This resulted in part from the fact that fascism, democracy, and communism fought on "world historical terms" that "legitimated forms of warfare that the liberal nineteenth century had tried to eradicate." Fascism and communism repudiated the liberal tradition and on principle advocated force and violence. Combined with various ethnic or nationalist animosities, this repudiation created wars of extermination, especially in Eastern Europe. The recognition that industrial output was critical to success in war had made industrial workers legitimate targets and helped erode the distinction between combatants and noncombatants. Whereas in World War I more combatants than civilians died, in World War II that ratio was reversed (Overy, 40; Roberts, 119, 131, 138). Noncombatants became targets also because it was thought, erroneously, that killing them, for example with bombing raids, would generate political pressure on their governments to surrender (Pape). (A version of this argument has been made by contemporary terrorists: as voters, civilians decide the government policies to which the terrorists object and can be targeted, they argue, as leverage for changing the policy).

With regard to violence and empire, humanitarian sentiment and conceptions of legitimate violence made coercive imperial policing increasingly difficult, even as the means of coercive force—through technological evolution or revolution—and the frequency of their application increased in Europe. Because indigenous people most often would not or could not stand and fight organized European forces, and in a tribal society the distinction between combatants and noncombatants is particularly difficult to sustain, Europeans had used exemplary atrocities to assert imperial control and deter rebellion. The moral revolution eventually made such a tactic almost impossible to employ, even when the indigenous who resisted empire employed similar violent means against imperialists and their indigenous supporters. In the late nineteenth century, it was possible to admit, with regret, the use of exemplary atrocity (Callwell, 41). A few decades later, the tactic could be used only covertly. As the rationale for imperialism became unbelievable, an important means to sustain it became unavailable.

3

Resistance

Resistance to European and then American power was almost instantaneous, but it was neither universal nor continuous. As soon as the Amerindians realized that the Europeans intended to conquer them, resistance began. Four hundred years later, Philippine resistance to Spanish rule immediately became resistance to American rule once it became clear that the Americans intended simply to replace the Spanish. In South Asia, the Europeans were at first more of a nuisance than a threat, certainly to the land empires and principalities of the region, but resistance to European power grew more or less in proportion as the threat from this power grew. At the same time, resistance was mixed with acceptance of trade and technology, even, in some cases, of religion. Europeans borrowed as well, and both Europeans and natives made new hybrid ways of life out of their partial, mutual, if wary, acceptance of each other. Some of the indigenous did not resist at all but tried to profit from European rule, either economically, politically, or spiritually, thus assisting European strategies of dividing against each other those they sought to conquer and then control. Those who resisted most often did not do so continuously, fighting to their death or victory. But resistance forgone was not forgotten, and it flared in rebellions, riots, strikes, and countless individual acts of defiance. Perhaps it is most accurate to say that resistance, or at least resentment, was continuous, although not universal; that it was intermittently violent but not sustained; and effective enough to achieve independence only in the twentieth century. Throughout their imperial history, the Europeans lost battles but not their predominance—until it rather abruptly collapsed. (Recent analyses of small wars and asymmetric conflict point to the fact that the weaker party in twentieth-century conflict appears to have won more frequently as the twentieth century progressed [Merom, 4–5; Arreguin-Toft]). So why did resistance to European imperialism fail for so long and then suddenly succeed? The simple answer is that success came when the rationale for empire went. But it took much struggle and bloodshed for the lack of a rationale to become politically effective. Only as the cost of empire went up, raised by increasingly effective resistance, did it become clear that it was not worth paying. Two cases of resistance to British rule, in Ireland and Palestine, offer lessons about both the growing effectiveness of resistance to imperial rule and its waning rationale. The case of Algerian resistance to French rule illustrates and qualifies those lessons.

Irish Resistance

Methods of conquest and control used in Ireland beginning in the sixteenth century were used in other imperial struggles (Kiernan, 21; Lee). After the Irish rebellion ended (1921), the British sent to Palestine to deal with restive Arabs members of the disbanded Royal Ulster Constabulary, including members of the Black and Tans, an auxiliary force known for brutal methods. Some of them subsequently used waterboarding when interrogating Arabs (Hoffman, 21, 74). Yet at the same time, ideas developed in the Irish resistance spread across the globe to be adapted by others disaffected with European rule. Among the first conquered, the Irish were the first native group to resist successfully and win their independence. (The Americans were the first settlers to gain independence.) In doing so, the Irish became an inspiration and lesson for others resisting imperialism. Even Gandhi, who led a nonviolent struggle, looked to the Irish example (Townshend, 11; McMahon, 146–47, 154–57; Begin, 284; M. Evans, 60).

The Irish struggle of course was violent, a string of rebellions and violent actions culminating, in retrospect, with the Easter Rebellion of 1916, launched in awareness that the British were preoccupied with the war in Europe. Like so many other anti-imperial efforts, the rebellion was a military failure. The superior force of the British, which included artillery, overcame in a matter of days the combined armed republican organizations that seized buildings in Dublin and declared the independent Irish republic. It became a political success because the British court-martialed and shot, or in one case hung, the rebellion's leaders, strengthening Irish resistance and building support for republicanism. Recognizing this political reality, in 1917 the

British prime minister, Lloyd George, worked with Irish parliamentarians (members of the British Parliament) to develop an agreement for Irish home rule, already promised by a 1914 law put in abeyance by the start of World War I. This law, the culmination of the parliamentary and constitutional approach to Irish independence, was, in a sense, the parallel to the Easter Rebellion, which was the culmination of armed or physical-force republicanism. A convention met for months and developed a plan for home rule, but pressed by the need for troops to fight World War I, the British government passed a law to conscript Irish. This not only overwhelmed the convention's work, it set the stage for the republican party, Sinn Fein, to win 71 percent of the seats in the December 1918 election to the British Parliament, routing the previously dominant Irish Parliamentary Party. The republicans had declared during the campaign that they stood for independence and would not sit in Parliament. Instead, they convened in Dublin as the Dáil Éireann, Gaelic or Irish for the Assembly of Ireland, on January 21, 1919, and declared Ireland independent. Parliamentarians who had won refused to join them, as did the Unionists, who for the most part represented the Protestant population in the northern counties of Ireland.

On the day the Dáil met, armed republicans ambushed and killed two members of the Royal Irish Constabulary, apparently without coordinating the action with Sinn Fein. The Dáil then authorized the armed republicans to become the Irish Republican Army (IRA). The IRA spent the next months stealing weapons, in desperately short supply despite efforts to get them from the Germans, and trying to free its members held prisoner by the British. From this point the conflict escalated through attack and reprisal on both sides. Although some republicans thought that the IRA ought to wage a conventional war against the British, the republican leadership had learned from the experience of 1916 and waged a guerrilla conflict, as the Dáil worked to establish an effective alternative administration to the British government in Ireland. The guerrilla action consisted of ambushes and assassinations, each side targeting the other's police, military, and political personnel. The IRA proved particularly adept at killing British intelligence officers and agents. The British punished the Irish population and burned civilian property while the police and their British auxiliary forces abused suspects, prisoners, and civilians. Some IRA prisoners went on hunger strike, resulting in several deaths. The British declared martial law because as the violence escalated the Royal Irish Constabulary, largely a Catholic force, crumpled under the weight of IRA assassination and social ostracism by Catholic republicans, a growing percentage of the population. Two years of escalating violence resulted in stalemate, which led to a truce and eventually to difficult negotiations, the start of which were delayed by the insistence of the British government that the IRA decommission its weapons. The resulting treaty left Ireland a free state with dominion status within the British Commonwealth of Nations, a neologism replacing "British empire." The treaty allowed six northern counties, largely Protestant, to separate from the Irish Free State, which they did. The terms of this treaty being unacceptable to leaders of the IRA, a civil war broke out between them and the government of the Irish Free State, which the IRA lost.

This bare outline of a complicated story reveals actions and issues that recurred in later phases of the Irish struggle (martial law, hunger strikes, decommissioning weapons) and in the history of resistance to Euro-American empire. The most important of these issues was the relationship between military and political power. Republicans aspired to nationhood as understood in Europe, which meant having an army. But renaming various armed groups the "Irish Republican Army" did not make it one. Physical-force republicanism could not compete with the physical force of the British military. The republicans thus had to find alternative means of coercion. As had resisters before them, as far back as the Amerindians in the sixteenth century, the Irish adopted a skulking style of warfare, which violated European military conventions: the republicans snuck up on and killed people not readily identifiable as combatants. Critical to the success of this warfare was its political calculation. Republicans killed many Irish Catholics, their core constituency. Nevertheless, they maintained and even increased their popular support among this constituency because the Irish Catholics they killed were, or were held to be, working for or with the British. This political context excused, if it did not legitimize, violations of morality and the normal calculation that a political movement will not prosper by harming members of its core constituency. This might not have happened—at least not to the same degree—if the British had not played into the hands of the republicans by retaliating against not only those carrying out the attacks but the Irish Catholic population in general. This was a standard approach used by all imperial powers in such situations (facing enemies that would not stand and fight), again going back to the Spanish in the Americas in the sixteenth century. In Ireland, however, this use of force undermined the British political position. The Irish enhanced this effect by establishing an alternative government that slowly exerted control over or replaced the British justice and financial system. This alternative Republican government drew to itself the legitimacy flowing away from the British. The IRA also used coercion to intimidate and silence those Irish who opposed it.

It would be wrong to imply in the Irish case, or in that of any of the other anti-imperialist struggles, that violent resistance had the unquestioning support of all those who favored independence. The use of violence was always contested in resistance or independence movements, as was its acceptable and effective level. Indeed, over time, the use of violence could generate resistance to an independence movement, even among those it claimed to serve. This eventually happened to the Provisional IRA later in the twentieth century. Generally speaking, the greater the legitimacy of the overt political independence movement, especially in comparison with its clandestine military organization, the more likely was a resistance effort both to avoid an overemphasis on violence during its struggle and to succeed in establishing democratic institutions after independence. Of course, the character of the military leadership was critical. Not every revolution was fortunate enough to have George Washington as its military leader. (There was no Washington in Algeria.) In the Irish case, a significant difference between early- and late-twentieth-century republican violence was the strength and legitimacy of republican political leadership.

The Anglo-Irish conflict and those independence movements that followed in the twentieth century were political and military struggles in which politics proved most important and success required that force be carefully calibrated, even subordinated, to political requirements (colonial, domestic, and foreign). This was true for both sides because of the basic structure of these conflicts. The imperialists had a preponderance of physical force but a weak moral position. The anti-imperialists, for their part, had a strong moral position but inferior physical force. Political considerations took precedence for the imperialists because they could no longer use their physical force as freely as they had in the past. Political considerations were at the forefront for the anti-imperialists because they lacked the physical force necessary to prevail, at least at the beginning of their struggle.

The mismatch of physical force and moral justification in anti-imperial struggles resulted principally from the growing number of Europeans who by the twentieth century did not think empire necessary or legitimate. First, the argument for free trade meant that direct political control over other economies was not necessary for the metropole to benefit, as had been the argument of mercantilism, the reigning view when European imperialism began. Second, partly in response to this changed economic understanding, empire had to be justified as a way of benefiting others, as an act of noblesse oblige or a religious duty. This was the humanitarian revolution discussed in the previous chapter. But if those for whom the good was being done did not want that good done, was there a point in insisting on doing it? Perhaps there was for evangelical Christians, but this justification lost more general public force as the twentieth century wore on. Was there any reason to kill and be killed to impose that good? Imperial struggles came to seem unnecessary, at least to significant segments of political opinion in the imperial countries. Hence, the military means permitted to the imperial power by its own people, who ultimately paid in blood and gold, became fewer and fewer in proportion as the military struggle came to seem less and less necessary. A good illustration of this point is Winston Churchill. During World War II, when Britain was fighting for its survival, he authorized extreme measures. After the war, however, when a member of Parliament, Churchill acknowledged that Britain, having lost India, had no interest in Palestine. He also asked, "Are we just to drift on, month after month, with these horrible outrages and counter-measures, which are necessary but nevertheless objectionable—necessary but painful? How long are we to go on?" (quoted in Begin, 321). The outrageous British counter-measures, not unprecedented in imperial policing, were needed to hold Palestine, but as holding Palestine was no longer necessary, such measures were no longer acceptable.

Putting politics above everything was what the situation required, but it was not, in fact, what either the imperialists or the anti-imperialists always did. Imperialists, like others, were attached to their traditions. When Field Marshall Bernard Montgomery, who just after World War II was serving as chief of the imperial general staff, had a more politically sensitive approach to imperial policing explained to him, he replied testily, "I cannot follow such reasoning" (Jones, 138). Montgomery remained an advocate of physical force. In addition, throughout the twentieth century, the militaries of the imperial powers focused on the Great Power conflicts with Germany and the Soviet Union that most immediately threatened their independence and survival. As we see in the next chapter, this made it difficult for them to conduct the kind of military operations needed to blend with the political requirements of the anti-imperial struggle. When the anti-imperialists used clandestine organizations, it was easy for them to lose touch politically and misjudge the level and kinds of violence that would further their cause (Tucker 2012, 49–70). On both sides there was fear, hatred, mistrust, vengeance, and ignorance, all distorting judgment and overwhelming calculation.

In the Irish case, although it was often a close call, the republicans proved better able than the British to calibrate force and politics effectively. Their inferior physical force led the republicans, on balance and not without exception, to emphasize politics. Both this result and its tenuous and contested character among republicans were typical of anti-imperial struggles. Another reason the Irish proved better than the British at effective military-political calibration was that the republicans had better intelligence (Townshend, 58). An intelligence imbalance favoring the anti-imperialists was a structural or enduring element of anti-imperial struggles (Tucker, 2014, 127–35). This imbalance resulted from two factors. First, almost all British government targets were visible. They wore uniforms, lived in barracks, or worked in government buildings. In addition, Irish Catholics worked in the British administration. Some number of them, yielding to intimidation by republicans or acting in sympathy with them, provided the republicans with information. Second, the British had little support among the population (republican intimidation was again a factor here) and so found it difficult to get help from the population to identify IRA members and plans. Lack of intelligence on the IRA was one reason the British resorted to punishing the population, but retaliation created a vicious circle for the British: by increasing the population's alienation, this approach increased the difficulty of identifying the IRA, which in turn meant that British use of force would be indiscriminate and have further adverse political consequences. Something similar happened to the British in Palestine.

Jewish Resistance in Palestine

The structural or enduring characteristics of anti-imperial struggles explain why certain features of these struggles recur, and why anti-imperialists could learn from each other. Learning was possible, of course, not only because of the structural similarities in anti-imperial struggles but also because anti-imperial struggles were waged against the same imperial power. Facing the same enemy as the IRA had, the Irgun studied the Irish case to learn its lessons, while those members of the IRA who renewed the

violent struggle in the 1960s in turn read and learned from *The Revolt*, Menachem Begin's account of the role of the Irgun, the violent underground
organization he led during the struggle for a Jewish homeland in Palestine
(Begin, 59, 284; "John Bowyer Bell"). The lessons taught by *The Revolt* were
also apparently deemed useful by those who fought Britain's replacement.
At least that is what the presence of a copy of the book at an al-Qaeda training camp in Afghanistan suggests (Hoffman, 484). As I have argued, one
of the fundamental structural features of anti-imperial struggles was the
disproportion in the military strength of the two sides. Hence, a principal
lesson that Begin learned from studying the Irish resistance, as well as from
reflecting on the situation in Palestine, was the importance of balancing
political and military efforts. Whereas the Irish republicans struggled, from
the beginning through the final years in the 1990s and even beyond, to coordinate physical force and political republicanism, the Irgun, certainly in
Begin's self-congratulatory account, coordinated both aspects of its struggle
from the beginning.

Begin's central discussion of the political-military balance occurs when
he is recounting the Irgun's first attacks against the British when he became
the leader of the organization in 1944. As the struggle was about to start,
Irgun members debated whether to first attack and then publish a justification for the attack or to publish the justification for attacking and then
carry one out. Those who wanted to attack first argued that only in this
way would they get Jews and the British to pay attention to the reasons for
their resistance. Attacking first was also preferred from a military point of
view because it preserved the element of surprise. Yet the Irgun decided to
issue the proclamation before attacking, putting politics before force. Begin
explained why:

> We would have to carry out many operations. There would be suffering and we
> would be hounded incessantly. Consequently, it was our duty to elucidate the
> principles of the struggle and its aims. The world must know what we are fight-
> ing for. The people should know why they must be prepared, through our oper-
> ations, to endure recurring troubles. The youth must know why they are risking
> their lives. We knew too that our fight would not be only military. The relative
> strength of the oppressor and the rebels was out of all proportion. We should
> clearly have to weigh the scales with other factors. One of them would be the
> political factor. To be more precise, the fight would be a political one pursued by

military means. Consequently political explanation, clear and persistent, would have to accompany the military operations. (Begin, 44)

Begin is here offering his account of what I have called the political-military dynamic central to the anticolonial struggle. Political use of force requires justification, but in a situation when the balance of forces is as unequal as it was in the Anglo-Jewish conflict, political factors had to be given greater weight to balance the scales and make success possible. This was so even though, in Begin's view, Jewish existence was at stake (27, 41). He could not take for granted that all Jews would agree with this assessment or that, even if they did, they would further agree that this or that instance of violence was well calculated to help the Jews survive. In fact, the various organizations involved in the Jewish resistance disagreed on such questions, reflecting disagreements among the Jewish people themselves. For Begin, the emphasis on politics derived from or was correlated with an emphasis on morality, the justice of the Jewish cause. He claimed that the real reason the Jews prevailed, despite their material weakness, was their moral strength. The supremacy of moral forces was "the law of history" (60). To sustain this moral strength, every act of violence required sound justification.

In the passage quoted above, Begin speaks of weighting the scales with other factors. What were these besides the justice of the cause and political explanation? Begin summarizes the Irgun's approach by saying that political logic brought about its strategy and that good strategy led to victory. The political logic was dictated by the basic political situation: to control Palestine, the Jews had to get the British out of the country and the Arabs out of the way. Given the violence that had occurred between Jews and Arabs, the British justified their presence in Palestine by saying they were there to protect the Jews. Once it was clear that the Jews could defend themselves with armed organizations like the Irgun in Palestine, this justification lost force. This was one way that the Irgun got the Arabs or the Arab issue out of the way. The other was to avoid attacking or harming Arabs but to warn them that if they attacked Jews, the Irgun would retaliate (Begin, 48–51; on this point, consider Hoffman, 473).

According to Begin, the Irgun strategy to get the British out of Palestine had three components: destroy the prestige that the British relied on to control their empire; take advantage of the international situation; and exploit the position and condition of Britain after World War II (Begin, 51–58). (The last two components were similar to what the Irish did, rebelling during World War I and seeking aid from Germany. At least some Britons agreed that British prestige was what held the empire together [Sayer, 154; Hoffman, 247, 356, 368].) The Irgun attacked British prestige by conducting military operations against British targets and in a variety of other ways. For example, the Irgun arrested British officers, whipping and hanging some, in retaliation for the British whipping and hanging members of Irgun. Threat of retaliation did not prevent the British from hanging Irgun personnel. Yet in addition to enhancing Jewish self-respect, the hangings and other attacks on British personnel meant that British officers and officials had to retreat into "ghettos" to protect themselves, undermining their authority. The Irgun took advantage of the changed international situation by meeting with representatives of the newly powerful Soviet Union (similar to the Irish meeting with the Germans) but most of all by continuing their armed resistance, which created for the Soviets the opportunity to damage the British through supporting a resolution of the Palestine problem. (The Soviet Union was the first country to recognize the state of Israel de jure.) More generally, the Irgun sought to exploit the international situation by using violence. Attacks on the British brought the world's attention to Palestine, turning it into a glass house, as Begin put it, and that attention restricted the violence the British could use in response. "Arms were our weapons of attack," Begin wrote, "the transparency of the 'glass' was our shield of defense" (Begin, 56). The Irgun used this international attention to redress the balance of forces, but it worked only because of the moral revolution that had changed European and American opinion regarding empire. The holocaust of European Jews also created sympathy for the Jews in Palestine. Finally, the Irgun exploited British weakness after World War II. The British were overextended, their empire disintegrating. With India on the way to independence, the traditional rationale for British empire in the Middle East (protecting routes to India) lost meaning. By 1947, as noted, Churchill acknowledged from the floor of the House of Commons that Britain had "no real interest" in Palestine (322). The Irgun knew as well that Britain's ally, the United States, where Irgun representatives operated (63, 64), supported decolonization. This is why Begin wrote that after World War II, Britain "was confronted by a hostile power in the east and a not very friendly power in the west. And as time went on her difficulties increased" (56). (As we see below, this summary describes the French in Algeria as well.)

The political and strategic issues facing the Irgun indicate the complex problems a resistance movement has to deal with. They extend beyond deciding when and where to strike and how to justify military action, to relations with foreign countries and even to questions of organizational structure and method. For example, Begin tells of an Irgun member who had been openly associated with the Hebrew Committee in the United States; when he returned to Israel, he remained in the open for fear that if he disappeared into the underground, it might taint the committee and threaten its work. As a result, he was arrested (Begin, 64). Experiences like this led the Irgun to become more clandestine (109–12)—until, that is, circumstances changed and it was time for it to operate more like a conventional military force (354). All of these issues—strategic, operational, organizational—affect each other and need to be evaluated in light of the political situation and the ever-present "imponderables" (40), which are changing continually due to resistance actions and government responses. Begin's formula that resistance is a political fight pursued by military means is a shorthand summary of these complex, interrelated aspects of resistance. Force was critical; it brought attention to the cause and created political dynamics that could be exploited (50), but it had to be used judiciously and within a political and moral context.

Critical to the ability of the Irgun to act effectively in this complex situation was that its High Command controlled all its activities, both military and political. The High Command "considered general principles, strategy and tactics, information and training, relations with other bodies and negotiations with their representatives" (61). This unified command was the organizational expression of the Irgun's unified political-military strategy. The Irish case, on the contrary, is marked by the contending claims for supremacy by the military (IRA) and political leadership (Sinn Fein). Again, a similar dynamic is evident in the Algerian case.

The principal objective of coordinating force and politics was to win and maintain the support of the Jewish people despite waging a violent struggle that would bring them hardship. The Irgun, as was often the case with resistance movements, did not initially have the public's support. It had separated itself from the official trusted representatives of the Jewish people and initially appeared extreme or mistaken in its strategy. The Irgun had to win support by demonstrating its prudent use of force and concern for the people. A turning point in winning popular trust, according to Begin, was the brief period in 1945–46 when the Irgun and the Haganah, the "official" Jewish military force, were united in forcefully opposing the British. This showed, Begin claimed, that the Irgun had been prescient in its turn to force. Once established, the Irgun's popular support was another shield. The people gave the British no information about the resistance even though the resisters lived among them and they saw them going out to attack. "The people gave the underground what the country's natural conditions failed to give: cover. We did not hide behind trees; we were guarded by living trees. Otherwise we could not have fought, certainly could not have won. The depth of an open underground is measured by the sympathy of the people for its struggle" (Begin, 109). In other words, the more sympathetic the people are to its efforts, the less far underground a resistance movement has to go. Good political decisions gain and hold this sympathy; the sympathy allows a movement to be more overt, which in turn makes it more politically aware (Tucker 2012, 49–70). British countermeasures that affected all Jews, not just the terrorists, helped build support for the resistance. Although there were some informers, Begin was largely accurate in describing the support of the Jewish people for the revolt, a fact the British acknowledged (Begin, 109; Hoffman, 130). This gave the resistance in Palestine, as was the case in Ireland, an intelligence advantage that was a counterweight to British material superiority.

Before an anti-imperialist movement can have the support of the people, the people must see themselves as a people, as a group with interests distinct from those of the outsiders who would rule them. The commercial and ideational aspects of European imperialism aimed to transform into Europeans those whom force had subdued. Resistance to imperialism had to overcome this Europeanization. Religion played an important role in this effort. In the Irish case, as noted, Catholicism was a critical element in resisting English rule. Judaism played a similar role in the Irgun case. It may seem unnecessary to point this out, since the revolt in Palestine was a struggle for a Jewish homeland. But Zionism, the movement for this homeland, was a secular movement, so the role of Judaism should not be taken for granted. In Begin's account, religion functioned in two ways. First, he argued that the survival not just of Jews but of Judaism was at stake. Ethnic and religious motives combined to unify the Jews in Palestine (Begin, 40, 41, 88). Second, the coherence and operational spirit of the Irgun came from its members believing there was absolutely nothing wrong with their struggle, that it was both morally justified and fully legal, according to a higher or the highest law. According to Begin, this allowed its personnel to meet questioning by British patrols with equanimity. This sense of righteousness, what Begin claimed as the ultimate source of the Jews' power, need not have derived from Judaism, but it is clear that it often did. Begin quotes a young Irgun member addressing a British court: "I, a young Jew, facing the sentence of death, lift my heart to my God, and give praise and thanks for the privilege of suffering for my people and my country, and say with all my heart: 'Blessed art thou, O Lord, King of the Universe, who has kept us alive and maintained us and enabled us to reach this season'" (285; cf. 355, 358). Faced with an imbalance of earthly power, resistance movements—in Ireland, Palestine, and Algeria—have relied on a higher power.

The Fundamentals of Anti-Imperial Resistance

To succeed, resistance movements had to find means to counter the effects of the three aspects of imperial power: military force, commerce, and ideas. The primary means turned out to be guerrilla warfare, socialism, and nationalism, either secular or religious or some combination of the two. (Zionism was often socialist, as its kibbutz component indicates.) Nationalism meant not just a sense of national identity and unity, an issue to which we return after examining the Algeria case, but the notion that each nation had a sovereign right to determine its own future. Success required combining in various ways the means of anti-imperialism into a political-military strategy (political logic dictating strategy, according to Begin), carried out, if possible, by some unified political-military command that was able to slowly but surely attain recognition as the legitimate representative of the nation's right to self-determination. The recognition had to come from the nation and from some members of the international community to force the imperial power to grant that recognition and, eventually, independence.

The overarching requirement for the anti-imperialists was to find means to overcome Euro-American resource superiority. The anti-imperialists could only do this by organizing and extracting support, including political support, from their populations. This was difficult given limited extractive means (the anti-imperialists had at first no bureaucracy or legal system; like the Irish they had to invent or capture them) and the poverty of such populations. It was necessary, therefore, to get outside support. In both the Irish and Jewish cases, it came from Americans, if not from the American government. The imperialists, of course, also relied on their populations for their power. By the twentieth century the imperialists had hundreds of years experience perfecting the fiscal-military state while the anti-imperialists were beginning from scratch. As a mechanism for providing security and protection of individual rights in return for tribute (taxes), representative systems of government were an important part of the fiscal-military state. Representative government did limit and direct government power, however, so influencing the representatives and those who voted for them became a prime consideration not just for the metropolitan government but for the anti-imperialists as well. This is another way of explaining the predominantly political character of the anti-imperial struggle.

As a rough rule of thumb, during the resistance to imperialism tribal and tributary societies displayed the same characteristics they did during the imperial conquest (cf. Keddie, 482). During the conquest, as we saw, tribal societies were typically easier to conquer than control while tributary societies were easier to control than conquer. Tribal societies could not match the resources or organization of the imperialists. Tributary societies could. Thus, it was easier to conquer tribal societies, at least in the sense that acute warfare ended sooner or was not necessary in the first place. The effect of conquest on tributary societies, once achieved, was to put Europeans in the commanding, if now changed, positions of the established political, financial, and social systems that permeated tributary society before the conquest. This allowed the Europeans to keep control. No such systems existed in tribal societies, which explains their relative lack of organization and resources. Yet their lack of such systems made them immune to thorough subjection. Resistance in the form of chronic warfare could continue for a long time. The Araucanians (see chapter one) had no capital to seize and when threatened could pack up and move to fight the Spanish another day. When it came to resistance, the collective social structure of a tribe made it relatively easy for a charismatic leader to mobilize the tribe's resources. Differences might assert themselves within a tribe or between tribes during the struggle or when it ended successfully and there was no longer a common enemy, meaning that tribes could often not sustain resistance at levels necessary to overcome European control (Kiernan, 74). In tributary societies, the task of mobilizing resistance was more difficult initially because of the thoroughness of European control and the relative isolation of individuals outside these mechanisms of control. Resistance might ultimately be more successful, however, if the means of control could be taken back from the Europeans or alternative ones developed. Establishing a legitimate alternative or provisional government was thus often a critical step in successful resistance to Euro-American power. Either religion, nationalism, or both could mobilize populations in tributary societies.

Having extracted these generalizations from the Irish and Jewish cases we may illustrate, if not substantiate, them by looking at the long history of Algerian resistance to French imperialism. The method of resistance seen in the Jewish case was different from and more effective than previous methods of resistance. Its effectiveness, of course, resulted in part from the kind of imperialism it faced, which was different from earlier forms—physically weaker, morally less sure—an issue to which we return in the next chapter. Unfolding from the mid-nineteenth-century through the mid-twentieth-century, the Algerian case allows us to see how resistance developed and changed over time, first failing, then succeeding. The Algerian case also allows us to see the role resistance movements have played during the past century in Islam, the third Abrahamic religion.

Algerian Resistance

In 1830, the French invaded Algeria, nominally part of the Ottoman empire. They did so for gain; to spread Christianity; to defend their honor, supposedly insulted by an Algerian leader; and to distract themselves from domestic problems. They massed a fleet of hundreds of ships off the coast, disembarked troops, and rather quickly gained control of coastal areas. This was a continuation of the centuries-old process by which Paris had extended its power over space through time, and would continue to do so all the way to Southeast Asia. It was equally a compelling illustration of the mobilizing and organizational power of the European nation-state.

As the French took control in Algeria, they turned mosques into churches, as the Ottomans had turned churches into mosques when they conquered Constantinople. In the absence of effective civilian political control, the military pushed the occupation forward (M. Evans, 9). Resistance continued longest in the interior, where Algeria's tribes ruled. The principal resistance leader was Abd el-Kader, the charismatic son of the leader of a branch of the Qâdiriyya Sufi brotherhood. In 1832, he declared jihad against the French, rallied various tribes to the cause, and began to build the means of resistance. He tried to establish a centralized government based in his hometown. In addition, he bought weapons from British and even French dealers and hired European mercenaries to train his troops (Vandervort, 58), efforts undertaken by Indian princes before him. In 1834 he negotiated an agreement with the French by which they acknowledged his control of some territory. The agreement broke down, however, and fighting resumed, which initially, but not ultimately, went in Abd el-Kader's favor. In 1835, the French captured his hometown. Subsequently, the seat of his government was wherever he pitched his camp. In 1836, he fought the French in a pitched battle at Sikkak, suffering a serious loss. After that, in a typical pattern, he engaged only in hit and run attacks. Still, using guerrilla warfare, the resistance held its own against the French, confining their control to the coast for the next five years. During this period, another treaty with the French recognized Abd el-Kader's control of interior territory, but it too broke down and fighting resumed again. Abd el-Kader again declared jihad against the French. In 1840, the tide turned, as Thomas-Robert Bugeaud took command of French forces and changed how they fought.

Bugeaud brought with him to Algeria the French experience suppressing guerrilla fighting in France, in the Vendée (1793–96) and, less successfully, in Spain during the Peninsula War (1807–14). From these conflicts Bugeaud drew the lesson that intelligence was essential. One had to know the topography as well as the guerrillas did, and one had to know where the guerillas were, which one could find out by constant patrolling. This intelligence allowed a commander to ambush the guerrillas (Sullivan, 78–80). In addition, Bugeaud emphasized mobility and an operational tempo that would exhaust the guerrillas. He made this possible by using mules rather than his soldiers as pack animals. Constant French patrolling and raids disrupted tribal life, making it difficult to plant or harvest. The French seized whatever food they found in tribal areas for their own use, increasing their mobility as they decreased the tribes', and destroyed the rest, burning villages and crops and killing livestock (87). These methods were similar to those used by other imperial powers to fight tribal societies. For example, military commanders, particularly George Crook, practiced these tactics later in the century in the American west. The French also used a level of brutality toward all Algerians that roused opposition in France. Bugeaud carried on undeterred. On two different occasions, French troops lit fires outside caves in which Algerian civilians had taken refuge, suffocating hundreds. To critics of his methods,

Bugeaud responded that the natives only understood force (Vandervort, 68, 69).

Bugeaud's anti-guerrilla methods, under his effective and inspiring leadership, transformed both the French military and the struggle for control in Algeria. They forced some tribes to surrender and eventually drove Abd el-Kader into Morocco, where for a time he found refuge and a base of operations. French military and political pressure eventually got him and his followers expelled from Morocco back into Algeria, however, and in the face of mounting French material and numerical superiority, he was forced to surrender. Imprisoned for a time, he was eventually exiled to Damascus, where he lived on a French pension and later saved the lives of many Christians during rioting in the city.

As Abd el-Kader's calls for jihad indicate, Islam was a critical element in opposition to the French in Algeria, as it was in resistance to the French in West Africa, and indeed anywhere Europeans or Americans took control of Muslim lands (Robinson, 405–6; Peters; Motadel 2014). In West Africa, inspired by the reform movements sweeping Islam in the eighteenth century, Umar Tal led jihads first against infidels and Muslims whose religious practice he thought impure and then against the French. A member of a Sufi brotherhood, Umar attracted a band of students, or *talaba*, who formed the nucleus of his army, a model with contemporary resonance. Not only did Islam provide Abd el-Kader and Umar Tal the tradition of jihad as a mobilizing tool (Motadel 2012, 841, 843, 850), but in its Sufi brotherhoods it gave them a ready-made social structure from which to draw support. Furthermore, in the figure of Muhammad, Islam offered the example of a leader who combined political, religious, military, and economic (or commercial) power and authority. Not only did this example encourage unity of command, but it was also the kind of unity necessary to resist the trinity of powers Europeans brought to their empire-building. Finally, Islam has a powerful millenarian component, most obviously in the figure of the Mahdi, whose appearance signals the arrival of the final Day of Judgment "and the end of corruption and oppression" (Peters, 42–43; Motadel 2012, 842; Keddie, 481). Muhammad Ahmad, a Sudanese Sufi leader, declared himself the Mahdi in 1881 and organized resistance to the Ottoman-Egyptian rulers of Sudan. His movement survived his death, in 1885, and carried on against the British, failing only after a major defeat in a pitched battle (Omdurman,

1898). In Algeria, millenarian views persisted into the twentieth century, fueling ongoing resistance to the French up to the final confrontation in the 1950s. The notion of jihad endured as well, legitimating violence against the French. The Algerians who carried out the Philippeville massacre of French settlers in August 1955 chanted "jihad" as they killed French civilians (M. Evans, 39, 80, 140).

If Islam offered, and still offers (Tucker 2012, 84, 224–40), advantages to those seeking to mobilize resistance, it also presented problems. The Sufi brotherhoods helped Abd el-Kader and Umar Tal mobilize, but they also created divided loyalties among Muslims, as leaders of rival brotherhoods refused to cooperate with each other. Many Sufi leaders focused on spiritual issues and reached accommodations with European powers. This was true in India as well as in Algeria, although generally in India Hindus were more willing to accommodate British rule than were Muslims (Peters, 50). In other cases, Muslim religious figures, and other Muslims, enjoyed profitable commercial relationships with the French (as a merchant, Muhammad was a model here as well) and did not want to disturb them by resisting French power (Abun-Nasr, 128, 202, 205, 209). Both the French and the British were careful of their Muslim subjects and typically worked with religious leaders and supported Islamic institutions, such as sharia courts and the Haj, the annual pilgrimage to Mecca. The imperialists saw these measures as a way to control their Muslim subjects and to gather information about them (Motadel 2014, 2, 5–7). Furthermore, Mahdism may as easily result in a passive waiting for justice as in an active resistance to authority (Peters, 42–43). It may also be the case that the insistence on the oneness of God in Islam magnifies differences among Muslims, making cooperation more difficult. In any case, the different responses of Algerians to French power were fairly typical of responses to Euro-American imperialism. Many resisted, but many cooperated with or accommodated the imperialists. Some saw the Europeans, and later the Americans, as models of necessary modernization, worthy of emulation. Whatever the cause, differences among Muslims undermined Abd el-Kader's efforts against the French. Muhammad Ahmad also ran into opposition from Muslims. He dealt with this by declaring that those who opposed him were "kafir" or unbelievers and could be attacked. However, since this contradicted the traditional teaching that Muslims should not kill other Muslims, this claim elicited fatwas or religious rulings against the self-proclaimed Mahdi (Peters, 67–68, 70, 72). Abd el-Kader dealt with Muslim opposition in a similar way. He sought a religious ruling that those who opposed him had thereby lapsed from Islam, which would have removed the stricture against killing them. His request was refused (Abun-Nasr, 205).

The eventual defeat of Abd el-Kader might appear to vindicate Bugeaud's approach of relentless campaigning and brutal tactics. Resistance did continue after Abd el-Kader's surrender, however, until 1857, and even longer in the desert south, until the 1920s. Most important, as a recent account claims, Bugeaud's methods and the subsequent legal discrimination against Algerians, which was intended to ensure French control and advantage, created a lasting hatred of the French that meant resistance would never end (M. Evans, 16–17; cf. Horne, 35, 42, 54–55). Along with occasional rioting, smaller disturbances and everyday acts of resistance, larger-scale organized resistance recurred, in 1864, 1871, and 1881, which the French countered with brutality (M. Evans, 32, 36). Underlying resentment and anger burst into a rebellion following World War II. The end of the war raised hope that the Allies, which included France, would honor the principles of the Atlantic Charter (1941), self-determination among them, as they had pledged to do. This hope, along with hunger (1945 saw the sixth period of famine since 1903) and bitterness over French control of land, led to a demonstration in Sétif in May 1945. As police attempted to take nationalist banners from some of the marchers, a shot was fired, killing a young Algerian. This set off a riot that led to the deaths of Europeans. The French responded swiftly and, again, brutally, aided in some places by groups of self-organized European vigilantes.

The French managed to restore order, but the killing in Sétif and associated violence changed the situation. Nationalists increased their organizational and political efforts and found a receptive audience, including over 130,000 Algerians who had fought with the Allies during the war (Horne, 42). At a clandestine party congress in 1946, a minority argued unsuccessfully for armed action. The French government pressed reforms, but settlers continued to resist them. Rigged elections in 1948 deprived Algerian nationalists of the electoral gains they would otherwise have achieved. This gave impetus to a nationalist clandestine paramilitary organization, the Organisation Spéciale (OS), which began to carry out operations and prepare in earnest for a war of liberation. The French retaliated. With the help of loyal Muslims, they dismantled the OS in 1950, as election fraud intensified. Mohammed Boudiaf, a veteran of the OS, organized a meeting in June 1954 that led to the formation of the National Liberation Front (FLN), which carried out its first coordinated attacks on November 1, 1954. Beginning as a group on the margins of nationalist politics, the FLN eventually fought its way to preeminence by attacking both the French and other Algerian nationalists. The eight-year war of liberation that began in 1954 was a civil war among Algerians, therefore, many of whom fought for the French. It became in addition a war among the FLN's leaders over who would lead the new Algeria. Even in France, it took on the character of civil war, or something like it, as elements of the French military and like-minded civilians fought both the French government and Algerians in an open revolt and with clandestine terrorism. Finally, the conflict in Algeria became part of the global confrontation between the United States and the Soviet Union. All of these conflicts interacted with and affected one another.

One element that remained constant between the nineteenth- and twentieth-century Algerian resistance was Islam. Calls for jihad echo through the decades of French rule (Vikor, 174). One of the main currents of Algerian nationalism in the twentieth century was traditionalist, emphasizing Islam. In the 1930s this included efforts to purify Islam, reminiscent of eighteenth- and nineteenth-century reform efforts, and modeled on the Muslim Brotherhood in Egypt, founded in 1928 (M. Evans, 54). Islam's significance varied in the FLN, depending on which leadership faction had the upper hand, but it was important generally to the rank and file (117, 120, 127, 228–29). One woman involved in FLN terrorist attacks recalled her parents saying that the German invasion of France in World War II was God's revenge on the French for how they had treated Muslims (Horne, 185).

In other ways, both the social material of resistance and the means of mobilizing it changed over time. Initial resistance to French rule was tribal and based in the Sufi brotherhoods. Neither the tribes nor the brotherhoods played a role in the final war of liberation, however. Without intending to, the French had destroyed their influence by destroying their material basis. By making land ownership individual, rather than communal, as part of their effort to modernize Algeria and exploit its resources, the French undermined the basis of Algeria's feudal tribal life. After changes to the law, individual Algerians could sell land that had before been considered communal property. Many did. Communal, tribal life and the religious warrior leaders it generated, such as Abd el-Kader, lost significance. Ill-prepared for the more modern economy developing around them (e.g., commercial farming), many

Algerians, legally discriminated against, were impoverished. French legal changes and the commercial forces they encouraged pulverized Algerian society into what a governor-general of Algeria described in 1894 as "a sort of human dust" (Horne, 37). To manage the Algerians, who in rural areas continued to meet in village assemblies, the French employed Algerian administrators and tax collectors as intermediaries. Although often corrupt (35), this system of intermediary rule proved durable. When the FLN launched its campaign, it did not win immediate universal support in rural areas, or anywhere else for that matter (M. Evans, 117; MacMaster, 442–43). But over time it did manage to infiltrate and win over "the preexisting structures of peasant society," including the village assemblies (MacMaster, 442). It did this by persuasion; by establishing its ability to wound the French; and by intimidation, killing Algerians who opposed it and those working with the French (Horne, 112, 134; M. Evans, 173, 216–17). The FLN spilled much French and Algerian blood, mixed it with the human dust of Algerian society, and tried to build a new Algeria.

The image of human dust is arresting but not quite accurate. As noted, village assemblies continued to function. Because Algeria was a part of France, Algerians participated in politics in other ways as well, both at home and in the metropole. In addition, as in Ireland in the 1920s and subsequently, nationalism in Algeria expressed itself through a variety of cultural means: religion; Arabic and Berber literary and cultural revivals; traditional music; a scouting movement (Algerians were barred from the French organization); and sports clubs, particularly soccer teams. An entire soccer team participated in the attacks on November 1, 1954 (M. Evans, 113). The original leaders of the FLN came out of this nationalist cultural environment. They were also from rural areas and, with grade-school educations, better educated than the typical Algerian. A few had even been to secondary school (40–41, 54, 58, 71, 119). Nationalist organizations and thinking had already to some degree molded the human dust before the FLN appeared, therefore. The FLN took additional steps to mobilize the population (a radio station, newspaper, unions, student organizations, and eventually a provisional government), but what distinguished the FLN among nationalists was its commitment to violence as the principal way to carry out the struggle. Frantz Fanon, who was a member of the FLN, and whom I consider in more detail below, is famous for his emphasis on the violence necessary for liberation. He was not theorizing, merely describing and trying to justify what he saw around him.

The FLN approach to national liberation contrasted with the one described by Begin. The disparity in power between the British and the Palestinian Jews meant that a purely military fight would lead to Jewish defeat. The leader of the Irgun argued, therefore, that the Jewish fight for a homeland had to "be a political one pursued by military means." All violence was in service of political objectives and had to be calibrated to achieve them. Given the supremacy of the political for Begin, we might also say that he understood that the righteousness of the Jewish struggle had to shine forth in the morality of the means used to carry it out. This was necessary to win and keep the support of Jews in Palestine but also to win and keep the support of Jews and others outside Palestine. Keeping political objectives supreme and all violence evidently subordinate to them was critical to maintaining the moral appearance of the Jewish struggle and thus its support. This was the only way the Jews could overcome the physical superiority of the British. The FLN and its armed forces, the National Liberation Army (ALN), understood the basic character of the struggle as Begin did. They had to avoid set-piece battles with the physically superior French and rely on terrorism and ambushes. "The ALN had to make up for the asymmetry of forces through secrecy, speed, and surprise . . . to wear down their adversaries through destruction and harassment" while winning the support of the Algerian people as well as audiences outside Algeria (M. Evans, 175). In fact, however, violence was more important in itself for the FLN than it was for the Irgun. Begin argued that violence had to be subservient to the political ends of the liberation struggle and not become an end in itself. For the FLN, violence became in a sense self-justifying (117, 120, 230, 335–36). But it was not self-justifying for those on the receiving end. The FLN's violence drove many Algerians to support the French (230). With their information and help, the French proved effective at finding and killing ALN and FLN cadre, something the British were unable to do in Palestine against Jewish terrorists.

How, then, did the FLN win? In one sense, it did not. In strictly military terms, the French defeated the FLN. Goaded by the guillotining of its personnel and hoping to show its power and support prior to a UN meeting on Algeria, the FLN escalated its attacks in Algiers, the center of French power, starting in the second half of 1956. As the tit-for-tat violence escalated, the FLN decided to target all European civilians, including women and children, as they had not previously done. To stop the violence, the government turned to the French military. In forcing this fight, the FLN made an error. In effect, it was engaging in a pitched battle. Making Algiers the centerpiece of the war allowed the French to concentrate their forces and their resources. Relying on organization, thoroughness, and torture, the French developed good intelligence, which they used with brutal efficiency. They destroyed the FLN in Algiers. A variety of tactics, including fortified barriers to cut off the ALN from outside resources, and the brutality of the FLN and ALN meant that even in rural areas the FLN was losing the war (Horne, 219–20).

What saved the FLN was the French and the French Algerians. The French fought the war with such brutality, exemplified in their use of torture, that they lost politically and morally. The French people, and outsiders who had influence with the French, such as the United States, decided the war was not worth fighting. The longer it went on, the less support there was for it among the French. FLN violence also cost it support among Algerians, as we have noted. The difference, however, was that the FLN could kill Algerians who opposed it, intimidating many others, while the French would not use such violence against their own dissenters. The relatively few French and settler hardliners who refused to accept Algerian independence and carried out terrorist attacks against French targets came as close as any French got to the supposedly purifying and identity-forging self-immolation of the Algerians. These efforts by the French die-hards, however, succeeded only in removing any moral or political credibility that the settler cause had left. In a sense, the FLN could get away with murder on a vast scale while the French could not because the underlying moral balance favored it: the unquestioned right of self-determination meant that the FLN had a vast reserve of moral force to call on. It wantonly spent this force, but the French moral position, so strong in earlier periods of the empire, became so weak that it was quickly worn away, at least in the eyes of most people. The French won the physical but lost the moral and political contest. The FLN won by default. The underlying political-military dynamic of anti-imperialism saved the FLN from itself.

Anti-Imperialism: Identity, Economics, and Violence

Having surveyed three cases, we may now note some of the characteristics of resistance that affected the fundamental political-military dynamic. Three related issues—identity, economics, and violence—were particularly important to the anti-imperialist struggle, but they also continue to resonate in contemporary politics and conflict.

In order to mobilize the resources available to them—largely the indigenous people—the anti-imperialists first had to encourage, if not create, a sense of identity and common purpose among the people distinct from the one that the imperialists had encouraged. To do so, they appealed to a common religion or encouraged the use of ethnic sports, music, language, and poetry, setting up associations or organizations to support or organize these cultural activities. These associations and organizations became cover for otherwise prohibited political and even military organizing. Sports clubs were part of the Haganah's infrastructure in Palestine, for example (Hoffman, 9, 38). Religious institutions were used in the same way. Eventually, as the resistance became more open, the anti-imperialists would establish an "army," police force, and provisional government—the instruments of resource extraction that could gradually develop legitimacy. The resistance would also develop a foreign policy and a foreign ministry to lobby outside powers or to negotiate with the imperial power, which was always reluctant to talk, as it immediately gave legitimacy to the "bandits."

Economic thinking helped establish an anti-imperial identity because commerce and all the changes it wrought were critical to European and American imperialists' conquest and subjugation of the world (cf. Keddie). Criticizing these imperialist economic arrangements and changing them were means to mobilize and organize resistance. Some Irish republicans tried to revive more communal, and supposedly traditional, understandings of property (Townshend, 3, 27; McMahon, 138; English, 27). Sukarno, who led the twentieth-century independence movement in Indonesia, advocated a kind of Islamic socialism, distinguishing it from the capitalism of the Dutch imperialists who lost control of the country following World War II. For good measure, he claimed that it was a conception indigenous to Indonesia.

One of the clearest statements of how economics could establish an identity different from the imperialists was made by Frantz Fanon in *The Wretched of the Earth* (1961). Without offering any evidence or argument, Fanon contended that European wealth came from the colonies. Redistribution of this wealth back to the colonies was necessary as a matter of justice but also because the retreating colonialists had left their former colonies with only two options: remain part of the former colonial system, thereby sacrificing independence, or pursue autarchy, thereby forgoing economic growth. Remaining part of the imperial system would prolong the exploitation of the former colonies. Autarchy would lead to an impoverished independence because even though the fervor of anticolonial nationalism had led "men and women, young and old [to] undertake enthusiastically what is in fact forced labor, and proclaim themselves the slaves of the nation," sacrificing everything for the sake of the common interest, this fervor would not be sufficient and would not last (Fanon, 78). The international redistribution of wealth to the colonies should be accompanied by socialism in the former colonies, a domestic transfer of wealth, as "this will allow us to go forward more quickly and harmoniously" (78). The socialism he advocated for the former colonies would be distinct from that which was locked in a global struggle with capitalism, Fanon claimed. It would be something new and world-changing, something that would finally humanize the planet (79, 83). Fanon believed this new world could come to pass for two reasons. First, he thought, apparently on Leninist assumptions, that the dynamics of capitalism would compel attention to the former colonies as markets for excess production (82). Second, he believed the vision of a new humanized post-capitalist world would appeal to European peoples, to whom, in closing his argument, he addressed himself directly (83).

Fanon's understanding of the historical development of capitalism and its then contemporary workings may have been wanting, but his appeal to the humanizing sentiments of Europeans was well founded. As we saw in the previous chapter, the moral revolution of humanitarianism had changed European attitudes toward empire and the well-being of peoples in faraway places. Fanon was also correct in seeing that the revolutionary enthusiasm of anti-imperialism would not last. (One inevitably thinks here of Cuban efforts to harvest the sugar crop with revolutionary enthusiasm, which ultimately retained its appeal only to revolutionary tourists.) Generally speaking, when given the chance, most former colonial subjects seemed happy to remain part of the imperial economic system. In many cases, anti-imperial socialism in the new nations became an opportunity for favoring certain cliques through monopolies and other contrivances. The economic growth and improved education that occurred after imperialism raised expectations that one-party crony socialism frustrated, giving rise to anti-government activity. Similar conditions are cited currently as propelling young Muslims into Islamism, reformist or militant versions of Islam (Taşpınar, 78). It is also, ironically and unfortunately, a replay of what happened under imperial rule, as economic development raised expectations that cultural and political discrimination frustrated.

Fanon's appeal to the humanizing sentiments of imperialists was coupled in his book, perhaps oddly, with a justification, if not glorification, of the use of violence by the indigenous. Fanon argued that anticolonialism, the assertion of an indigenous identity, required violence: "When the native hears a speech about Western culture, he pulls out his knife—or at least makes sure it is in reach" (Fanon, 35). It was good that he did so, according to Fanon, because imperialism was violence, brutal unrelenting violence, and would yield only when confronted with greater violence (48, 57, 66). This was not only or principally a military issue. Fanon, who was a psychiatrist, thought that anticolonialism required above all a revolution of thought and feeling (36–37). Violence was essential to this revolution, even if an armed struggle was not necessary to achieve liberation. Violence would unify the nation, liquidating "regionalism and tribalism," and allow individuals to overcome feelings of inferiority created by colonialism: "Illuminated by violence, the consciousness of the people rebels against any pacification" (73, 74).

Although perhaps an extreme expression of the role of violence in antiimperialism, Fanon's argument was not idiosyncratic. Menachem Begin made essentially the same point ten years before Fanon in his account of the Jewish fight for Palestine. Begin declared "we fight, therefore we are" (Begin, 46). He insisted that such remarks were not hyperbolic because the holocaust, under way as he and his colleagues and other Jews struggled for Palestine, showed that the alternative to fighting for Palestine was extermination. But fighting was also necessary to restore Jewish self-respect (27, 41, 59, 217, 338). At one point in his narrative, Begin referred to the Jews under British control as slaves, a term Fanon had applied to all colonized people (112). At another he remarked, "the world does not pity the slaughtered. It only respects those who fight. . . . All the people of the world knew this grim truth except the Jews" (36). Begin claimed that the British disdained the Jews and did not believe they could carry out a successful armed struggle (31; Hoffman, 99). Jewish resistance showed this view to be false, according to Begin. By restoring Jewish self-respect, resistance strengthened Jewish identity and helped forge the settlers and immigrants into a Jewish nation

(Begin, 194–95). This is one reason Begin could claim that even failed military operations could be political successes (52).

Begin and Fanon's arguments about violence help explain something evident throughout anti-imperialism, from the Irish case forward: the strong commitment to violence, even when it seems counterproductive politically. In underground or clandestine organizations like the Irgun, disputes with other resistance organizations or internal factions often come to dominate strategic calculations. Because violent action is the reason for such organizations, it is easy for these disputes to occur over the proper role of violence, with factions escalating violence to outbid rivals for support (Tucker 2012, 50–70). Begin and Fanon point to another reason violence escalates. It increases even at the risk of the political objectives it is meant to serve because it is undertaken not for political but for psychological reasons. As I have argued, controlling violence helps beget success. Its psychological importance highlights the difficulty of such control.

Given the horrific kinds and levels of violence and calls for jihad in late-twentieth- and early-twenty-first-century anti-imperial struggles, we might suppose that religion is responsible for excessive or politically counterproductive violence. Yet the century of Hitler, Stalin, and Mao and the example of Rwanda should make us reluctant to conclude that horrific levels or kinds of violence require religious inspiration. Nor should we assume—with the examples of the Thirty Years' War and Christian calls for holy war (Firestone; M. Larson) and more recently the violence of Hindu nationalism in mind—that Islam alone among religions is prone to violence. Fanon's *Wretched of the Earth* suggests that something else may be at work in the horrific violence of recent anti-imperial struggles. His appeal to humanitarian sentiments sat uneasily beside his glorification of violence, not only because humanitarianism and violence seem to contradict each other. Humanitarianism, doing good for others, as I argued in the previous chapter, also became part of the rationale of imperialism. A thorough rejection of imperialism, of the thinking that justified it, would seem to require the rejection of humanitarianism, therefore. To be thoroughly anti-imperialist one must be thoroughly inhumane. To be consistent, one should also reject socialism and nationalism, both imperial exports. The claim made by Islamists that Islam alone, particularly a supposedly pure version antedating contact with Europeans, is the one answer to all of life's questions is such a thoroughly anti-imperial view. It would combine easily with violence similarly unrestrained by any hint of European humanitarianism. Such an approach would also have the practical advantage, when applied to one's fellow Muslims, now declared *kafir* or apostates, of encouraging their slaughter, thus putting an end to Islam's factionalism by killing off factions. (Others such as Abdullah Öcalan or Velupillai Prabhakaran took a similar approach at the beginning their anti-imperial campaigns, killing any rivals to their leadership.) Even at this extreme of human action, however, imperialism's opponents may not have escaped the power of European thinking. Could we not say of Hitler, Stalin, and Mao that each in his own way anticipated the Islamists and showed kinship with them by seeking to escape the limits of bourgeois European humanitarianism in order not to return to a supposedly purer past but to reach a supposedly better future?

Those resisting imperialism had to learn how to do it successfully. Leaders of successive anti-imperial struggles learned from those who had gone before. They quickly ascertained that they could not match physical imperial power. What took longer to learn was how—through what means and methods—to nonetheless succeed. Skulking or guerrilla warfare proved insufficient. Eventually, anti-imperialists discovered how to combine guerrilla warfare with moral and political warfare. This new approach exploited the Euro-American moral revolution and the fading rationale for empire. In the context of the changed geopolitical situation in Europe, especially after World War II, this new approach allowed anti-imperialists to prevail more often than they had before.

4

Retreat

The strategy and tactics that Bugeaud used in Algeria were used throughout the Euro-American conquest: pursue the dispersed enemy relentlessly with mobile columns and destroy what could not disperse: crops and settlements, often including the noncombatants who tended the crops and lived in the settlements (Vickery, 312, 317; Colby). These two tactics were connected; even the most mobile pursuit might fail to find the enemy and end up with nothing to do but burn crops and settlements. Campaigning through Florida in 1818 against renegade Indians and runaway slaves, Andrew Jackson's forces often failed to find the enemy but still did much damage to him by burning his villages and crops. Following the conquest of India and during their efforts to dominate parts of Africa later in the nineteenth century, British imperial warfare was more and more tribal warfare, the kind that Jackson waged in Florida. Toward the end of the nineteenth century, British officers began compiling the various lessons they had learned in such fighting. One of the most famous of these compendia was Colonel C. E. Callwell's *Small Wars: Their Principles and Practice* (1896). Callwell expressed straightforwardly one of the essential tactics of imperial policing: "The most satisfactory way of bringing such foes to reason is by the rifle and the sword, for they understand this mode of warfare and respect it. Sometimes, however, the circumstances do not admit of it, and then their villages must be demolished and their crops and granaries destroyed; still it is unfortunate when this is the case" (Callwell, 41). A professional like Callwell preferred to take the fight to the enemy and meet him in open battle, with gun and sword, rather than to chastise him with an exemplary atrocity. Open battle was more honorable and might be decisive, as were the battles of Omdurman (1898) and Umm Diwaykarat (1899) against the Mahdist forces in Sudan. But like all Euro-American imperialists, the British knew that in imperial policing or small wars the most honorable course was not always possible.

As we have seen, the Irish war of independence (1919–21) began with an ambush of the Royal Irish Constabulary, and the British responded to the skulking or guerrilla tactics of the Irish with the same tactics they used in other parts of the empire when confronted with such warfare. They were not successful. Nor in the 1920s was imperial policing going so well on the northwest frontier of India, the tribal lands of what is now Pakistan (Moreman, 114–15). Six years after the Irish war ended, a British officer, Major B. C. Dening, published an article in a professional military journal describing what he called the "Modern Problems of Guerilla Warfare." Dening reflected on his experience on the northwest frontier. First, he noted that guerrilla warfare had changed little in history. For the Great Power, victory came through mobile columns using good intelligence to hunt down the enemy. Dening then noted, as Winston Churchill did after his own time on the frontier, that guerrilla wars "have always been carried out with the utmost ferocity on both sides" (Dening, 348; Kiernan, 70). (Dening did not mention that the British also bought the loyalty of certain tribes, keeping these clients under control and, through them, other tribes as well [Tripodi]).

Having outlined the historical pattern of guerrilla warfare, Dening argued that it had come to an end. Four things had changed: communications, moral sentiment in the imperial powers, imperial resources, and guerrilla firepower. The combination of global communications and increased sensitivity to the treatment of imperial subjects meant that the imperial powers could no longer police their empires with their accustomed ferocity. Knowledge of such ferocity traveled quickly back to the metropole. The exemplary atrocity was no longer exemplary. It was simply an atrocity, which metropolitan populations would now not abide. Dening may have been thinking here of the Amritsar massacre (1919), in which a British general ordered soldiers to fire on a crowd of Indians (the soldiers were Indians), as well as events in Ireland. Other Britons had such events on their minds (Sayer). With their own atrocities, guerrillas could goad the Great Power into excessive use of force. "Political propaganda," Dening wrote, would ensure that a reciprocal use of force by the Great Power would merely "draw blood upon [its] home front" (Dening, 349). The French experienced this difficulty in Algeria. In addition, as Begin later argued too, the guerrillas had learned that overextended empires (this did not include the United States, according to Dening) were vulnerable to exhaustion. Prolonging the campaign and attacking economic targets exploited this overextension. The first example of such an approach occurred in the Cuban insurrection (1895), Dening noted. The lesson was learned and subsequently applied by anti-imperial forces in both the Boer War (1899–1902) and Ireland (1919–21). Finally, technology had advanced so that small, easily hidden and transported weapons (automatic firearms, high explosives) could do great damage, "particularly in large centers of population" (350). In the northwest frontier of the British empire in the early twentieth century, weapons or the money to procure them came from the Arabian peninsula across the Gulf of Oman (Kiernan, 70), as they continue to do in the early twenty-first century.

Prevented from arguing for more ferocity by the change in moral sentiments at home, Dening contended that the only way to meet the modern problems of guerrilla warfare was to increase intelligence and mobility, the latter through such technologies as "mechanical transport" and wireless. Thus, the new technology supposedly revolutionizing acute warfare among the Great Powers after World War I in Europe would, Dening thought, revolutionize chronic warfare as well. In addition, as a replacement for ferocity, the Great Power had to consider removing "the main causes of grievance upon which the insurrection relies for sustenance" (Dening, 351). This was not always possible, however. In such cases, the Great Power should announce to both the rebels and its own population the policy to which it would firmly adhere. Why this would do any good given the problems he had outlined, Dening did not explain, but this advice made him an early example of the military's insistence on having what came to be called an "end state" against which it can plan (Tucker 1997, 114–24). Finally, the status of the military force should not be left vague. "As soon as disturbances increase," the Great Power should declare martial law. Dening concluded by stating his belief that "by modern developments, guerrilla forces had gained more than the forces of the Great Powers" (Dening, 351).

Although focused on tribal warfare and drawing particularly on the experience of warfare along India's tribal frontier, Dening was pointing to developments occurring throughout the empire, indeed around the globe. His reference to the danger posed to population centers and his concern with the effect of political propaganda in the metropole, for example, both show that the worry was not just tribal areas. Nor was the moral revolution confined to Great Britain, even if it was more advanced and politically effective there than anywhere else. Dening also noted a global phenomenon of growing importance in the empires: nationalism (Dening, 348). He made too little of this phenomenon, however, perhaps because in tribal areas it was less important. Almost by definition, despite their centrifugal tendencies, tribes exist as more or less cohesive social, political, and even economic units, ready for further mobilization and organization. This was not so in nontribal populations, those we have described as tributary. Decades or centuries of rule by upper castes or by Europeans and their foreign ideas and religions, and the subsequent social and economic disruption caused by integration into global commerce, left indigenous people in tributary societies without a clear identity or cohesive nonimperial social and economic organization. Giving the indigenous an identity was necessary to mobilize them, as the Irish, Jewish, and Algerian resistance movements demonstrate. Nationalism proved indispensable in these efforts. Nationalism was the functional equivalent of tribalism. It was even better than tribalism, however, because it was compatible with a large, even industrializing, society. In any event, as Menachem Begin pointed out, once the insurgents forged a sufficient degree of cohesion and support among the people, the people could become the cover and concealment for the guerrillas or insurgents that topography gave tribal forces in their rural homelands (Begin, 108–9).

Despite failing to recognize the political and military importance of nationalism, Dening in effect captured the core of what later in the twentieth century came to be called counterinsurgency doctrine. The purpose of this doctrine was to replace the tried and true methods of imperial policing and small wars, the mobile column and the exemplary atrocity. As insurgents mobilized the people and through persuasion and coercion turned them into camouflage, cover, and concealment, they no longer needed to operate in dispersed mobile groups that imperial mobile columns could pursue to exhaustion. The insurgents could disperse in place, so to speak, among the people. The moral revolution in Europe and America and changing attitudes toward imperialism meant that imperialists could no longer with impunity destroy the human cover that protected the guerrillas. The counterinsurgents thus needed to develop alternative tactics and strategies. These slowly coalesced into counterinsurgency doctrine. Technology would play a key role in this doctrine, as a way to increase mobility and lethality. In place of the exemplary atrocity, counterinsurgents would argue, as Dening did, for redress of grievances and political work to counter the mobilizing efforts of the insurgents. These countermobilization efforts would peacefully remove the human cover the insurgents needed by winning people—their hearts and minds, in the standard phrase—away from the insurgents and to the government side. As the campaign for hearts and minds progressed, good intelligence gleaned from the people now giving their support to the government would allow the imperialists to target the insurgents with precision, minimizing damage to the people that the government was trying to win over. Finally, another point only hinted at by Dening in his call for a clear policy, the doctrine would call for the coordination of military and political means and authority, as neither addressing grievances nor outlining a clear, defensible policy and pursuing it in the face of an insurrection is simply a military matter.

While the need for the new approach and its basic outline appeared in the 1920s, successive efforts to develop and implement it effectively over the next nearly 100 years proved difficult. The difficulties arose from several related causes. First, for a host of reasons, ways of operating embedded in institutions do not change easily (Tucker 2006; Jones). Strapped for resources and focused on events and then looming war in Europe, the imperial powers did not think through in any systematic way or develop the means to deal with the consequences of the changes that Dening and others had indicated. The British, for example, turned to air power in the Middle East to handle insurrection in the territories they acquired there after World War I. Resource-efficient technology was the answer in this case, not time and resource-intensive efforts to understand the people and address their grievances. The U.S. Marines compiled their colonial policing experience in a *Small Wars Manual* (1935; revised 1940) but then, anticipating war with Japan, set it aside to devote their limited resources to sorting out how to conduct the opposed amphibious assaults necessary to capture islands for naval and air bases in the Pacific. After World War II, the context of empire changed as the newly dominant powers, the United States and the Soviet Union, worked to dismantle the remnants of European empires and extend their competing *imperia*. The European imperial powers did not have the resources or, it turned out, the will to resist these new powers or their own restive imperial subjects. The contest between the United States and the Soviet Union came to dominate defense and security thinking as the European retreat from empire gathered pace. Planning, equipping, and training for major war between the Great Powers was paramount, dealing with insurgency a secondary issue. (This logic prevailed before World War II as well [Moreman, 108]). In the United States, insurgency remained a secondary issue despite the declaration of the Kennedy administration in 1962 that "subversive insurgency ('wars of liberation')" constituted "a major form of politico-military conflict equal in importance to conventional warfare" (quoted in Tucker 2006, 52–53).

The problem with counterinsurgency doctrine and practice arose from more than just the circumstances in which the Euro-Americans tried to implement them. At the most basic level, insurgencies tended to arise in states that were incapable of dealing with them. Arguably, if a colonial regime or a newly independent nation were good at identifying and redressing grievances and identifying and arresting insurgents, then the insurgency would not have gathered power in the first place. Colonial regimes did not exist, however, to respond to indigenous aspirations. From the beginning, they existed to impose European control. This did not change, even when the rationale for empire became to civilize or democratize. Furthermore, as Dening indicated, some grievances, even if identified, could not be redressed. After World War II, for example, the demand for the imposition of Marxist regimes in the colonies was not negotiable because the Euro-Americans considered those regimes evil in themselves and a threat to Euro-American power elsewhere in the world. At least in the case of the European empires, the Europeans controlled the colonial administration and could make unilateral decisions about how to organize and respond to insurgencies. The situation was different for the United States, which had to work with newly independent governments. When these governments insisted on control over the counterinsurgency effort, they often proved inept or inclined to use an unacceptable level of coercion. If they allowed the United States to take the lead, they appeared subservient and lost legitimacy.

If the colonial regimes existed to impose European control, one would think that they would at least have been good at identifying and arresting insurgents. The colonial regimes were not police states, however; far from it (French, 248, 252; Hoffman, 356, 479). The insurgents then had an initial intelligence advantage over the government. As noted in the previous chapter, the government, its personnel, and key political and economic infrastructure were all visible and initially vulnerable to the insurgents while the insurgents were typically unknown to the government (Tucker 2014, 127–60). Unguided by good intelligence, the government's responses to insurgent violence were initially not discriminate enough. They targeted those not involved in the insurgency, which made winning hearts and minds more difficult. But if the government did not win the support of the people, then it did not get their help, such as obtaining information on the insurgents. This in turn led to more insufficiently discriminate targeting, setting up a vicious circle. Contributing to this circle were the inertia of conventional military thinking, which values the application of force; frustration at the slow and uncertain results of the hearts-and-minds approach; and in some cases, a desire for revenge for losses inflicted by the insurgents. In Algeria and some other settler colonies, excessive violence was the result on both sides of an almost primordial fear and hatred.

The information failure characteristic of most counterinsurgency campaigns was not simply a problem of lack of operationally useful intelligence on the enemy. Winning the hearts and minds of the people meant convincing them that the government could protect them and would allow them to flourish. In the midst of a violent insurgency, protection or lack of it is evident. More difficult to convince people of is the long-term beneficial intent of the government. Given the demands of fighting an insurgency, evidence of this beneficial intent is likely to be equivocal, especially in the eyes of those the government has long ignored. As well as beneficial action, persuasion on this point requires speaking to the people in a language they understand—presumably their own—in a way that respects those things they most esteem. A shorthand for the knowledge of what people esteem is "cultural knowledge," a term heard frequently, mostly to decry its absence, as the United States struggled with insurgencies in Iraq and Afghanistan early in the twenty-first century (Flynn et al.).

Critical to success in a counterinsurgency, according to doctrine, cultural knowledge proved hard to acquire and even more difficult to act on. "Cultural sensitivity," if it is a human trait, is evidently not evenly or widely distributed. Military forces do not normally select or train to encourage it. Units had to be established to specialize in "cultural" work (Special Operations Forces in the United States, for example). Even when these forces managed some level of cultural sensitivity and language ability, they survived as near orphans in military systems that valued force above all (Tucker and Lamb, 69–106). Nor were civilian imperialists necessarily more likely to possess cultural knowledge and sensitivity. Again, the whole thrust of imperialism was not to understand the "other" but to control and reshape it. When those in the field did possess cultural knowledge, leaders in the metropole often ignored it or saw it, paradoxically, as one more tool by which they could force metropolitan culture, whether Christian or liberal democratic, on their imperial subjects (Tripodi).

Counterinsurgents often tried to break the vicious circle of ignorance and violence by using more coercion, simply ignoring the hearts and minds approach. Dening noted the problem with using coercion: metropolitan populations would not abide it both because of their humanitarian sentiments and empire's lack of rationale. The only way to use more coercion, then, was to hide it, which Great Britain managed to do in Kenya, for example. At roughly the same time, the French were unable to do this in Algeria. Modern communications and sentiments, and the lobbying of nongovernmental organizations (increasingly numerous in the decades following World War II), made hiding coercion more difficult as time went on. The United States discovered this when its supposedly secret prisons and interrogation techniques for terrorists became public. (For an alternative to "hearts-and-minds" counterinsurgency that did not rely solely on coercion, see Shafer, 127–32, and Leites and Wolfe.)

Yet it is also possible to exaggerate the limitation on coercion. Broadcasting images of government violence, even the inadvertent killing of civilians, into living rooms does not automatically turn people against a counterinsurgency or counterterrorism effort. Thorough analyses of these issues show that the connection between media reports of violence and public reaction is not a simple one (Larson and Savych 2006; Larson and Savych 2005; Berinsky). What particularly shapes public reaction appears to be the public's sense of whether the counterinsurgent or military campaign has a sound rationale. This in turn hinges on the degree of agreement or disagreement about the campaign among domestic opinion makers, including leading politicians (Kingdon, 2002; Entman, 2003). If opinion makers disagree, the public will begin to doubt the usefulness of the military engagement. One reason that the French were able to pursue their post–World War II imperial ambitions for so long was the agreement across the political spectrum that it was the right thing to do. The French government also maintained an ability to control the press that did not exist in Great Britain or the United States. Still, the moral revolution and a preference on practical and principled grounds for letting people sort out their own affairs was the frame, in the now current term, through which public opinion in Euro-America saw empire during the imperial retreat. French and American efforts to emphasize the geopolitical threat from communism did not displace this frame. The failure of those endeavors worked against both imperialism and efforts to save or reinvent it.

The final general problem with counterinsurgency doctrine and practice was that it called for a unity, or at least a coordination, of military and political action that proved difficult to achieve. Dening argued that it was best to declare martial law early, so as to free the military from the constraints of civil law and allow "systematic operations." Declaring martial law, however, is a politically unwelcome step, signaling the depth of the problem, undermining the government's claim that its opponents are mere "bandits," and acknowledging that a rebellion is under way. Instead of martial law, the imperial powers took other approaches. The British tended to declare emergencies and impose emergency regulations, which "allowed them to suspend civil liberties wholesale . . . [and] to apply coercion with little or no discrimination." The French gave "hegemonic power to the army to control operations" (French, 249). The French and British could take their respective approaches because they were the civil power in their colonies. Neither approach regularly attained the smooth, balanced coordination of political and military measures that doctrine called for. Carrying out counterinsurgency in places where they were not the civil authority, Americans never resolved problems of coordination. Their military and civilian authorities carried on separately, except in those cases where an ambassador and a general managed to work together or, for a short period in Vietnam, when an organization was given both civil and military authority (CORDS, Civil Operations and Revolutionary Development Support, 1967–73). Yet, even in this case, the problem remained, since CORDS focused on only one aspect of the conflict: the so-called other war for the hearts and minds of the Vietnamese.

Different considerations explain the critical failure to better coordinate military and political action. A fundamental one, connected to the rise of imperialism, is worth mentioning here. The imperial powers became imperial powers in part because, like other modern states, they developed specialized government agencies. First, and most important, they developed finance and war bureaucracies, which together constituted the fiscal-military state (described in chapter two). The logic of this state was that its financial department raised money so that its military department could spend it in war. The financial department then repaired the damage to the state's finances so that the military could again wage war. As specialized agencies, neither department concerned itself with the activities of the other. Furthermore, in liberal states, which conceived themselves as having objectives higher than mere violent acquisition, warfare came to be seen as a kind of exemplary atrocity writ large, a regrettable necessity, almost an aberration, to be conducted with overwhelming force so as to make possible a return to peace, the presumed natural condition, its violence justified only by the greater good it was presumed to do. Together the institutional arrangements of the fiscal-military state and the preferences of the liberal state encouraged a sharp division between civil and military authorities, one not easily overcome in situations, like counterinsurgency, that called for uniting the civil and the military.

Affecting all of the imperial powers, the institutional and political separation of the civil and the military was perhaps most pronounced in the United States. America came into existence declaring itself a new order of the ages. Among other things, this declaration meant that America would be different from Europe, an old world mired in cynical balance-of-power politics, in which one could barely distinguish between peace and war, since both served the acquisitive desires of monarchs and aristocrats. A strong tradition has existed in the United States of insisting on the separation of the civil and the military and on the supremacy of the former, and not merely as a legal matter. When the War of 1812 began, James Monroe in effect resigned his office as secretary of state, since until the war ended he did not think he would have much of importance to do. Although past middle age, he wanted to get into the fight, as any self-respecting republican gentleman would have. When the war ended, he returned to the planning and administration of the country's foreign affairs (Ammon, 313, 348). One would think that planning for the future as the ongoing military campaigns unfolded, maintaining a consistent policy, as Dening called for, and thus the duties of the secretary of state would be important to gain the maximum benefit from the investment of blood and treasure required by the fighting. Yet for Monroe, policy and force seem to have existed more or less in separate worlds. (For more recent examples of this American attitude among both military and civilian leaders, and some commentary, see Tucker 1997, 117–20.) It remains the case that the first and only institutional point in the

U.S. government at which the political and military come together is the presidency (*Forging*), a long way from the villages where hearts and minds are won. The specialization of the fiscal-military state made empire possible but defending it difficult.

The cases of France and the United States illustrate how these general problems with counterinsurgency manifested themselves. The British were once thought to be the best at counterinsurgency, having had the most experience and the greatest success. More recently, British reputation has suffered, following failures in Iraq and scholarly critiques (e.g., French; Ledwige). Long before their current problems, however, the British, recognizing that they were no longer able to hold their empire, more or less decided to give it up (French, 251). This means that for understanding the fate of empire amid modern conditions, the British case is not the most exemplary. The French, by contrast, tried desperately to hold on to theirs, as a way to recover from the debacle of defeat in 1940 and the Vichy government that followed. Unlike the British, the French also developed a theory of counterinsurgency to support their efforts. This theory and French attempts to apply it reveal more than the British case does about the fate of empire and the peculiarities of insurgent or irregular warfare. The Americans also devised a theory from which they derived counterinsurgency doctrine, a theory that sought to justify, according to American principles, the assertion of American power in the newly independent states created from colonial possessions. This theory, in various modified forms, continues to shape and influence the American response to the challenge of Islamic insurgency.

The French

Almost immediately following the Japanese surrender that ended World War II (September 2, 1945), the French began fighting Vietnamese communists (known as the Vietminh), led by Ho Chi Minh, to regain control of Indochina, which they had lost during the war to the Japanese. Ho, who had spent most of his life prior to 1945 outside of Vietnam, and his colleagues declared Vietnam independent on the day Japan surrendered. No country recognized the new People's Republic. Negotiations with the French dragged on, as the Vietminh fought with other nationalists to dominate the struggle for Vietnamese independence. Negotiations having failed, the communists declared war on France in December 1946. The war lasted until 1954. The French had technological superiority (armor and aircraft) and gained some initial success against Vietminh forces, which had serious deficiencies in training and leadership. However, as the French continued to seek out and engage their enemy, the Vietminh dispersed their forces, denying the French the decisive battles they sought. When they thought it was to their advantage, for example against weak outlying garrisons, the Vietminh engaged the French, operating in battalions, regiments, and divisions as expedient.

Confirming a trend noted by Dening, the Vietminh under Chinese guidance followed a strategy of prolonging the war, in expectation that the French would not be able to sustain their effort (Zhai, 704, 709; Chinh, 162, 191). (Ho had translated Mao Zedong's "Protracted Warfare" into French [Zhai, 695].) To ensure their own endurance, the Vietminh undertook intense efforts to mobilize and organize the Vietnamese people. They established a parallel administration to the official colonial one and extracted resources from the people through persuasion, propaganda, and coercion (including exemplary atrocities against Vietnamese and French). In the areas they controlled, and eventually throughout the north after the French withdrawal, the Vietminh also undertook land reform and reeducation: confiscation and redistribution of land, execution of class enemies, and internment in forced labor camps (Logevall, 151, 172, 632–33). During the course of the war, French Union forces (French and colonial troops) suffered 92,000 dead, 114,000 casualties, and 28,000 captured. Many of the dead, injured, and captured were from France's colonies, but the steady grind of the war without apparent progress wore down public opinion in France. Support for the war dropped from 52 percent in 1947 to only 7 percent in early 1954. When the fortress of Dien Bien Phu fell to the Vietminh in May 1954, following a well-planned siege and conventional assault, with several thousand more French casualties and many more taken prisoner, the French were forced to give up their Indochina colony (Fall, 34, 40, 105; Larkin, 240; Rioux, 217; Logevall, 170, 273).

The defeat at Dien Bien Phu deflated French confidence. Coupled with the Suez disaster of 1956, it marked the contraction of French (and British) power and exposed the fractious ineptitude of the government of the Fourth Republic. Insufficiently funded and supported by its political masters, the French army felt betrayed, setting in motion events that would help bring about the end of the Fourth Republic in 1958 and an attempted putsch against Charles de Gaulle in 1961, following his decision to grant Algerian independence. Together, Dien Bien Phu and Suez marked the end of European imperialism.

The defeat also sent the French army, or at least some of its officers, in search of an explanation. How could a small, backward colony have imposed an unprecedented defeat on its metropolitan master (Logevall, 534)? The answer began to emerge in meetings and training sessions even before the war in Indochina had ended (Géré, 129; Ambler, 398). It appeared in the pages of professional military journals shortly after Dien Bien Phu, as the French began another war, this time for control of Algeria, an integral part of France. The explanation for their defeat was that the French had encountered a new kind of warfare—revolutionary warfare. Unlike classical warfare, in which one military force sought to defeat another in order to gain control of territory, revolutionary warfare sought to control a territory by controlling its population. That was the point of Vietminh efforts to organize the Vietnamese people. The decisive fighting of the war took place not on the battlefield, where the French had the advantage, but in the hearts and minds of the Vietnamese and French (in Indochina but above all in the metropole). The Vietminh's strategy of protracted warfare was aimed ultimately not at the French army but at the French people. Ruthlessly mobilizing and organizing the Vietnamese people into a revolutionary weapon made the protracted war possible.

The Vietminh organizing effort had two components, according to the French. One was political warfare. The Vietminh infiltrated all sections and levels of Vietnamese society through a system of committees. These committees paralleled the official political organizations (hamlet, village, province, etc.) and included a series of social committees (of the young, the old, women, etc.). The result was a system that, according to Charles Lacheroy, a French student of revolutionary warfare, allowed the Vietminh to take physical possession of people. But this component—political warfare—was not sufficient. The second component of revolutionary warfare was psychological warfare. The Vietminh aimed to take control of people's hopes and fears, loves and hates—to take control of people's souls. (In this way they were trying to counteract the effect of liberal democracy and Christianity, the component of Euro-American imperialism that aimed to shape people's minds and souls.) To do this, they used a variety of measures ranging from propaganda to brainwashing, supported by physical punishment. The Chinese had advised the Vietnamese to "reeducate" even prisoners of war, both French and Vietnamese, before releasing them (Zhai, 703). The French referred to these measures as psychological warfare. Political warfare and psychological warfare together produced revolutionary warfare. Guerrilla warfare overcame superior force by avoiding it when it was concentrated and attacking it when it was dispersed. Revolutionary warfare, even as it employed guerrilla tactics and other forms of physical coercion, went beyond them. It avoided superior force by targeting the thinking of the enemy and its supporters, which, in a democracy, we may say, is always dispersed. To avoid such dispersion or differences of opinion on its own side, the revolutionary forces crushed freethinking through propaganda and coercion and destroyed its social-material basis by confiscating wealth and property. Revolutionary warfare had allowed the Vietminh to beat a force that by conventional measures was superior (Lacheroy, 312–22). Thus, revolutionary warfare was itself a revolution in warfare.

Having diagnosed the problem, French officers knew the remedy. The French military had to transform itself by adopting the techniques that had defeated them. In so doing, the army "was thinking only of turning against an enemy the arms that he used," explained a French officer. "What could be more normal in war?" Otherwise, the army would simply fail to adapt itself to the kinds of struggles it would face in what he called the "era of the masses" (Planchais, 11). Although discussion of how to respond to revolutionary warfare began during the Indochina war, the French fought the war there with conventional military tactics and an older approach to colonial warfare, the oil-spot technique, which the French had developed in Africa in the late nineteenth century. This technique called for moving from a secure to an insecure area, securing that and then moving on, using political, economic, and military means (protection from Vietminh attacks, hunting the Vietminh) to win over the local population. Insufficiently resourced and never wholeheartedly embraced, the oil-spot technique still managed to produce some success in southern Vietnam (Logevall, 632–33). These and other more conventional efforts proved unavailing overall, however. Failure in Indochina convinced some French officers and civilian leaders that revolutionary warfare was a new and decisive form of conflict requiring a revolutionary response.

The French account of what beat them may rightly be criticized for not sufficiently acknowledging the contribution of Chinese material aid and strategic advice to the Vietminh victory. Indeed, a critic might contend that the French account of revolutionary warfare did not fully admit the conventional character of their military defeat. Such criticisms were later made of those who blamed insurgency for the American defeat in Vietnam (Summers). But if it is true, as the old saying has it, that amateurs talk of strategy while professionals talk of logistics, then the French account was the more professional. The Vietminh army depended on thousands and thousands of civilian porters (14,500 in the Dien Bien Phu campaign). It could not have fought its conventional campaigns without them, any more than it could have sustained the war in general without careful attention to human resources. Revolutionary fervor, even among the military units, was not spontaneous. Reading accounts of the war, one sees that the Vietminh were in good measure operating as armies did in the preindustrial world. Vietminh soldiers covered about as much ground in a day (twenty miles) as the best infantry of that olden time (Logevall, 239, 393, 404; Landers, 220, 205). Vietminh trenching to besiege Dien Bien Phu would have been familiar to any eighteenth-century general. These old techniques worked, however, only because of the modern methods of revolutionary warfare that mobilized the Vietnamese population. They made the Vietminh victory possible.

As the conflict in Algeria grew, so did support among both French military and civilian officials for measures to respond to revolutionary warfare. (The meeting in Geneva that led to the partitioning of Vietnam and the withdrawal of France ended in July 1954; the war in Algeria began in November 1954.) The result was a belief that to be effective, any response had to address the mind of the enemy (psychological warfare) as well as the minds of its own citizens and allies (psychological action). The French, like the Vietminh, would use coercion, reform, and propaganda to control the bodies and souls, the hearts and minds, of their enemies. The military took much of the initiative in establishing its new way of warfare, setting up courses and other training. It also established staff offices to handle psychological warfare and psychological action, the latter to dispense information within France. It deployed psychological operations units to Algeria, whose job it was to influence, if not control, the thinking of the Algerian people (Ambler, 218; Géré, 182, 193–94).

Civilian decision makers supported the military's new approach. The French minister of defense, Maurice Bourgès-Maunoury, published an article in 1956 in the *Revue Militaire d'Information* presenting the new French doctrine. He acknowledged that France was undertaking a policy of reform in Algeria but insisted that these reforms not be seen as concessions to the terrorists. They were not a sign of weakness but of the strength of France's longstanding commitment to Algeria, a commitment that made failure there unthinkable. He described France's army in Algeria as an army of pacification, a term the Spanish had used to denote their efforts to secure their control of Mexico and Peru (Elliott, 40). The army thus had a new role, which he said reflected the evolution of the military art over the preceding twenty years. This new role was necessary because the rebels in Algeria were practicing revolutionary warfare. Therefore, France could no longer have an army only of soldiers. It had to have an army of builders, doctors, and pioneers as well, an army of propaganda and an army in contact with the population (Bourgès-Maunoury, 6–7). The struggle in Algeria was over the loyalty of the Algerian people; the key to victory was not defeating an enemy force or seizing territory but winning that loyalty.

In July 1957, the chief of the French general staff approved and Bourgès-Maunoury, now prime minister, signed a directive on psychological action. It argued that atomic weapons had changed both warfare, by making it almost unthinkable, and politics, by increasing the burden of fear that the average citizen had to support. This implied that government should act to help its citizens bear this new burden. It asserted that France was on the side of those struggling for freedom in the world. It presented psychological action and warfare as the necessary responses to revolutionary warfare, which it characterized as a way of war "permanent, universal, and total." It went further than this, claiming in effect that all of warfare was psychological because "the final end of military operations was of a psychological order" and that "man, in his heart and spirit, is the essential objective of war and of psychological action" (*Instruction provisoire*, 30, 39, 41). To prevail against the threat of revolutionary warfare, the government and the military had to win hearts and minds in France and overseas. The directive discussed at length the required tactics, techniques, and procedures of psychological action and psychological warfare, carefully distinguishing the two (one used against enemies, the other with friends) and what was permitted in each.

In November 1957, several months after the directive appeared, the commander of the army corps in Algeria presented it to France's allies at a meeting at Supreme Headquarters Allied Powers Europe (SHAPE). The presentation to SHAPE gave a detailed analysis of the geopolitical situation, dwelling on the struggle between communism and freedom in the world, the advance of communism toward world domination, and the betrayal of

France by some of its allies (the United States and Great Britain), who recently had sent arms to Tunisia, arms that the French were certain would end up in Algeria. The advance of communism, the presentation argued, was occurring by an indirect route made necessary, in part, by the presence of nuclear weapons on both sides, which made traditional large-scale warfare too risky. The presentation avoided detailed discussion of tactics and techniques. Like the directive, however, it presented revolutionary warfare as the key threat to freedom in the world and argued that the objective of this kind of warfare was not control of territory, as was the case in conventional warfare, but control of people. Therefore, psychological warfare was central to the defense of freedom and the West (Allard, 10, 19–21, 39).

The French effort to implement their new doctrine ran into the expected difficulties. Many in the French military did not accept the doctrine because it cut against what they understood to be the core of the military profession, which was to close with and destroy enemy forces, not ingratiate oneself with a civilian population. In addition, many officers, reasonably given their recent history, were not persuaded that revolutionary warfare posed a greater threat to France or the West than the armored forces of the Russians and their allies sitting 500 miles to the east (Tucker 2006, 19–22). In addition, of course, the new approach to colonial resistance in Algeria or the older oil-spot approach in Vietnam did not succeed. Even if better resourced or more thoroughly implemented, they were unlikely to have. Despite having some indigenous sympathizers, the French faced colonial populations that were in general antagonistic to their control, even without the prompting of the Vietminh or the National Liberation Front (FLN). The French did reform their colonial administration and offered degrees of local control within a French Union, but such efforts proved too little and too late. The French did not grasp the depth of the resistance they faced; neither, with exceptions, did they have sufficient respect for those they ruled. To this extent, and in other ways, the French did not have the cultural sensitivity or the other resources that the new doctrine required, even though the United States provided a great deal of material support. Given this overall situation, and the ingrained tendency of the military to see force as the answer, it was almost inevitable that force, including torture, would predominate in the French response. In the short term, at least in Algeria, given the mistakes and brutality of the FLN, this worked, but in the long-term, given the moral revolution in Euro-America, it did not (M. Evans, 275–76).

The French experience countering insurgency raised another crucial question about their new approach. In both Indochina and Algeria, civilians ceded control to the French military. This gave the military a political role, reinforced by the doctrine of psychological action, which made it the job of the military to influence domestic opinion. These developments, along with the sentiment among some that the military must guard the republic from the misrule of feckless politicians and a dispirited, distracted people, led to a deep politicization of the French military and eventually the attempted coup of 1961. The response to revolutionary warfare was not the sole cause of the politicization, but it contributed significantly. If revolutionary warfare was "permanent, universal and total," seeking control over the souls of friends and enemies, and the remedy had to be as comprehensive, then its politicization, even to an anti-democratic extreme, should not have come as a surprise.

Seeing the problems of French counterrevolutionary warfare, one might wonder whether an alternative to the French approach existed. Was the French diagnosis right; if so, was their treatment the only one? Considering only the guerrilla portion of revolutionary warfare, we would conclude that the French were wrong in thinking they faced something new. Opponents of European power had been using guerrilla tactics for centuries, since almost the first contacts in North and South America. Nor did Mao, Ho, or other advocates of revolutionary warfare believe that the developments Dening had noted (modern communications, small powerful weapons, and the growing effect of the moral revolution) mean that modern guerrilla warfare could achieve decisive results by itself (Mao 1961, 55, 62). Indeed, Mao wrote like the most conventional of Euro-American commanders, "It is only by attack that we can extinguish our enemies and preserve ourselves" (105). Romantic, or as Mao might have said, subjective, fantasies about the power of guerrilla warfare were for infantile revolutionaries, like Che Guevara. Mao argued that victory would come through conventional military means, as it did in fact in China and Vietnam, against both the French and the Americans.

Considered as a whole, however, the French were right to conclude that revolutionary warfare was something new in the history of anti-imperialism. It was a technique, its proponents claimed, that allowed the weak to overcome the strong by moving from guerrilla warfare fought with almost no weapons or military skill to a conventional military victory. The key was to protract the conflict, which would give time to change the balance of forces by wearing down the imperialist and building up the political strength and conventional military force of the anti-imperialist. The critical element of this strategy was to mobilize and organize the people (Mao 1967, 50–51, 88–89). Once mobilized, the people would provide unyielding material and spiritual support to the revolution. Popular mobilization was the foundation of the revolution because it was the only way to make a cohesive force out of the dust into which years of tributary and then imperial rule had ground the people. Nationalism, cultural as well as political, was an essential means of mobilization to break the hold of colonial thinking and extract the resources necessary to carry out the struggle. Grouping all nationalists in the same political organization, or popular front, was an effective tactic, one used by both the Chinese and Vietnamese communists. Almost as important was the appeal to "progressive forces" in the metropole and around the world as a way to undermine support for imperialism.

The new revolutionary warfare approach to combat imperialism developed over decades. One might even say centuries because protracted warfare was a version of the chronic warfare that developed on the fringes of empires. Popular mobilization was the new element, giving resistance the kind of cohesiveness that tribes enjoyed. Protracted warfare, therefore, required the development of nationalism not only as an idea but as a practical reality achieved through reviving traditional language, music, customary religious practices, and other cultural institutions, as in Ireland and Algeria, or through newfangled committees and revolutionary reeducation, as in Vietnam. As a practical matter, it also required a good deal of coercion applied to the indigenous people, plus the slow but steady, decades-long process of learning how to organize clandestinely and manipulate both the population at large and the various organizations and institutions that gave shape to and ruled people's lives.

Ho Chi Minh was part of the decades-long process of learning how to organize and manipulate. In the years when he was away from Vietnam, he worked as an agent for the Comintern, the international component of the Russian communist party, and learned through trial and error about revolutionary organizing. In these years, he maintained contact with Irish and Korean nationalists and revolutionaries (Logevall, 4, 11) and worked as an organizer in France, Russia, China, and Southeast Asia. Mao had of course also been part of this process. His writings, while based in Chinese experience, were a kind of anti-imperialist counterpart to the imperial policing guidebooks or lessons-learned compendia that appeared in Great Britain. (Mao knew the history of anti-imperial struggle, even as he stressed that the Chinese revolution was "a new military process" [Mao, 1961, 95].) We have seen elements of what the French called revolutionary warfare in both the Irish and Jewish struggles for independence. Menachem Begin's principles of anti-imperialist resistance contain many points made by Mao: the importance of the people, the role of violence in forging their identity, the possibility of exhausting the imperial power, and the need for clandestine organization and a transition to conventional military activity, as well as the centrality of politics to the military struggle (Begin, 44, 61, 354, 357; Mao 1967, 9, 10, 32, 35, 39, 71; Mao 1961, 55, 62, 89). Begin came out of the eastern European/Slavic revolutionary (originally anarchist) underworld where Ho worked and much of the tactical repertoire of conspiratorial revolutionary mobilizing first developed (Hoffman, 104, 105, 208–9). Nor was revolutionary warfare an inherently Marxist or Leninist strategy, as Begin's example reveals. It could be and was used by rightists, democrats, and leftists. A democrat like Begin respected pluralism, limited the use of force, even against the enemy, and emphasized persuasion. Marxist-Leninists like Mao and Ho stressed unity, used pluralism or nationalism (the popular front) only as a tactic, imposed centralized control of thought and property under a leader or a ruling party, and were more willing to use violence, stressing, for example, the need to eliminate enemies and traitors (Mao 1961, 69, 87, 111; Chinh, 206; Beckett, 81). The Leninists distinguished themselves from rightists, whom they otherwise resembled, by claiming that their revolution was not only permanent and total but universal, because it fought ultimately for all mankind.

In sum, an unfavorable balance of forces imposed certain tactics and strategies on all engaged in the anti-imperialist struggle in the twentieth century, as they had in past centuries. Within the genre of anti-imperialist struggle, however, revolutionary warfare was something new—permanent, total, and universal. Mobilizing the people allowed chronic warfare to move from the fringes to the heart of the colonial possession, using the people as cover and concealment, the sea in which the revolutionary fish swims, according to Mao (Mao 1967, 93). Further developments in communications and weapons brought it—in the form of terrorism—into the heart of the metropole. Al-Qaeda and Islamic State have mobilized people to carry out attacks in Europe and the United States.

Although their analysis of revolutionary warfare contained a hard kernel of truth, the French had a hard time convincing anyone of it. The British took a less theoretical view of the whole business, one based in their long experience in imperial policing (French, 1–5). The Americans thought the French approach just a clever way to explain why they should hold on to their empire. In addition, over time, countering the French view that revolutionary warfare was universally effective was the difficulty revolutionaries had in replicating the success of Chinese and Vietnamese revolutionary warfare in other parts of the world (Beckett, 81–84). (Mao warned of this problem [Mao 1967, 82].) This raised the question of whether the threat justified the extreme countermeasures the French proposed. Furthermore, even if the communists treated nationalism as a mere tactic, other anti-imperialists saw it as essential. Could imperialists, then, use nationalism to help defeat communism? It was also the case that French recourse to a permanent, total, and universal response did not sit well with Anglo-American notions of limited governmental power, freedom of speech, and strict subordination of the military to civil authority. Finally, the anti-democratic tendency of the French approach contradicted the claim made to SHAPE that the new French way of war was necessary to defend freedom and the West.

Although the United States rejected the French diagnosis and treatment, it did assume the mantle of defender of the West, the Free World, which was implicit in the French appeal to SHAPE. It also came eventually to recognize that insurgency and guerrilla warfare were problems that it had to deal with. It sought a way to do this that was compatible with America's political traditions and sense of history, or its understanding of the westward course of empire.

The Americans

In the briefing to SHAPE, the French tried to get the Americans to take up the torch of counterrevolutionary warfare. The Americans declined the honor. The briefing took place during the Eisenhower administration, which acknowledged the Soviet threat but sought to defend Euro-American empire (the West) by emphasizing nuclear weapons, not counterrevolutionary warfare. The administration feared the consequences for the economy of military spending. It operated on the assumption that the more the government spent, the less the economy would prosper. Enduring economic growth came not from government spending but from private initiative, an opinion which was a faint echo of the faith in human initiative that helped

launch European imperialism. It held as well that a dynamic private economy, hindered as little as possible by government, was essential to the freedom at the heart of the West. Eisenhower feared that the confrontation
with the Soviet Union, if not managed properly, would threaten freedom in
the United States by forcing the government to violate these basic principles of political economy. (Eisenhower's Farewell Address is a brief, elegant
statement of his views.)

Eisenhower's apprehension was grounded in America's history. Like
other modern states, the United States had developed the mechanisms of
the fiscal-military state that had allowed Europe to project its power over
the world. It had never needed those mechanisms to operate to their full,
however, because unlike European states, the United States had faced no
persistent external threats until almost the middle decades of the twentieth
century. Before then, the end of each of America's intermittent wars had
meant a return as quickly as possible to a small peacetime defense establishment, a reduced tax burden, as debt payment allowed, and a weak national
government. Given the Soviet threat, such an approach was no longer possible. The United States now needed to be on a permanent wartime footing.
The fiscal-military state or the military-industrial complex, as Eisenhower
called it in his farewell address, would have to assume a bigger role in American life, Eisenhower feared. One way he and his administration dealt with
this fear was to seek the most economic military strategy. Such a strategy
would mean lower taxes, less government interference in the economy, and
thus both greater freedom at home and a sound defense of freedom abroad.
Nuclear weapons, therefore, became one of the key elements of the administration's strategy because they provided more bang for the buck, as the saying
had it. Nuclear weapons would deter Soviet aggression, making more expensive army divisions unnecessary. The administration understood the danger
posed by Leninist subversion. It sought to counter it with covert action carried out by the newly formed Central Intelligence Agency and by psychological warfare (Mitrovich). Early successes in fomenting or assisting coups
in Guatemala and Iran seemed to confirm that the agency was a cheap and
effective way to deal with revolution, whether nationalist or communist.

The Eisenhower administration's strategy had its critics. They believed
that relying on nuclear weapons and covert action did not give the United
States enough flexibility to respond effectively to the range of problems
confronting the country. For example, was it really possible to think that

the president of the United States would use nuclear weapons to deal with conventional military problems such as the Chinese threat to Taiwan? How would the United States respond to the unrest and insurgencies occurring in the former colonies gaining independence after World War II? Was covert coup plotting a sufficient response? If it was doubtful that the United States would use nuclear weapons to defend Taiwan or defeat a Maoist insurgency, then nuclear weapons were not a credible deterrent. Beyond such strategic arguments, critics questioned the premises of the administration's approach. Would government involvement in the economy necessarily limit economic growth and imperil freedom? Even Eisenhower agreed that increased spending during a recession or depression could stimulate economic growth. Was there not, his critics asked, a set of government actions beyond this that could help the economy reach its full potential? If so, then the Eisenhower administration had been constrained by false dilemmas (Friedberg, 88–93, 139–40).

The election of John F. Kennedy brought the critics of the Eisenhower administration to power. The new administration was ready to pick up the torch. Indeed, in his inaugural address, the president declared that it had passed to a new generation. This generation did not believe in the dogmas of the quiet past. It believed instead that the economic policies of the federal government could unleash the full potential of the American economy, making funds available for new domestic programs and a national security strategy flexible enough to deal with the array of security problems, including revolutionary warfare. This was the administration that declared counterrevolutionary warfare to be as important as conventional warfare, and it took steps to implement this view. In a special address to Congress in May 1961, Kennedy discussed the problem of insurgency, as he did when he addressed the West Point graduating class in 1962. On the latter occasion, he spoke of the need for "a whole new kind of strategy, a wholly different kind of force," to meet the threat of insurgency (Kennedy, 226.) The administration also issued policy directives; established new organizations, both on the National Security Council and in the Department of Defense; intervened to promote officers sympathetic to its objectives; and had administration officials visit military installations to emphasize the importance of its new approach. The president met with high-ranking military officers and singled out the U.S. Army Special Forces for attention (Tucker 2006, 52–54). This was the "wholly different kind of force" Kennedy had spoken of. Unlike other military forces, Special Forces was not intended to close with and engage enemy forces. Originally established to train indigenous personnel to fight behind the lines of advancing Russian forces in Europe, Special Forces was now to work with indigenous populations and train indigenous military forces, so that together they could overcome revolutionary warfare.

The thinking behind the administration's approach to countering revolutionary warfare was fully expressed in "United States Overseas Internal Defense Policy," National Security Action Memorandum 182 (cited below as NSAM 182). Issued August 24, 1962, about seven weeks after the Algerian Declaration of Independence, the policy in many respects was similar to what the French had proposed five years before at SHAPE. "Subversive insurgency," according to the memorandum, was "a most pressing U.S. national security problem" and would remain so for the foreseeable future (NSAM 182, 1). Over decades, the communists had developed effective techniques for mobilizing and organizing people. Using these techniques, they were now poised to take over the new nations emerging from the ruins of European imperialism. In effect, NSAM 182 argued that just as organizing the people inside a nation turned them and the nation's resources into an effective weapon against the metropole, so too would organizing these new nations, their resources, and manpower, turn them into an effective weapon against the West. This was the objective of the Soviet Union and China. Nuclear weapons inhibited the resort to conventional warfare; the danger of escalation to a nuclear exchange was too great. Instead, the struggle between freedom and tyranny was now taking place in what had heretofore been peripheral areas, in the new nations of the southern hemisphere.

In each of these nations, the memorandum insisted, the "ultimate and decisive target is the people. Society itself is at war and the resources, motives and targets of the struggle are found almost wholly within the local population" (NSAM 182, 8). To prevail in the struggle, then, to overcome the threat of subversive insurgency, required that the new governments of the new nations win the support of their people. This in turn required that these governments address the people's grievances and aspirations. "The causes of insurgency . . . stem from the inadequacies of the local government to requite or remove popular or group dissatisfactions" (6). Repression, the memorandum warned, could only buy time (4). The key to success was using this time to build the capacities of the new nations to meet the needs of their people and thus win their support. This meant not just building the capacity of the new governments but, in effect, mobilizing to counter the mobilization effort of the communists. Just as the communists used political, social, economic, and psychological measures in addition to coercion to organize people, so too must the new nations—and so must the United States, to support them.

The memorandum stressed several times that the United States could not do the work of the new nations; it should only assist. Various U.S. government agencies could provide different types of assistance. For the Department of Defense, not just Special Forces, this meant developing capabilities far removed from its traditional role of engaging enemy forces. As one of the architects of the new approach, Walt W. Rostow, deputy special assistant to the president for national security affairs, told a group of foreign officers at their graduation from a U.S. Army counterinsurgency training program in 1961:

> You are not merely soldiers in the old sense. . . . Your job is to work with understanding with your fellow citizens in the whole creative process of modernization. . . . [Y]ou take your place side by side with those others who are committed to help fashion independent, modern societies out of the revolutionary process now going forward. I salute you as I would a group of doctors, teachers, economic planners, agricultural experts, civil servants, or those others who are now leading the way in the whole southern half of the globe in fashioning new nations and societies that will stand up straight and assume in time their rightful place of dignity and responsibility in the world community; for this is our common mission (Rostow 1961, 237).

This language was similar to that used by the French minister of defense in 1956. Of course, instead of hoping that the new nations would one day take their place as reliable partners in the French Union, American officials were looking forward to reliable partners in the United Nations.

Yet the American effort to manage the retreat from empire differed from the French approach in significant ways. For one thing, the memorandum accepted that not all insurgency was communist led or inspired. It cited Algeria as an example of a nationalist, not communist, resistance movement. Therefore, the United States had to look at each case individually "in the light of [U.S.] interests." It could not "assume a stance against revolution *per se*" (NSAM 182, 12). A violent revolt in certain cases might be in the interests of the United States. More generally, the American approach was based on the idea that a revolution was occurring in the world, the revolution of modernization (3). As Kennedy's defense secretary Robert McNamara argued, this revolution would produce discontent and violence, even in the absence of communist subversion (Shafer, 80). The point of the U.S. approach was not to deny or stand against this revolution but to recognize, understand, and lead it, or the nations affected by it, toward freedom rather than tyranny.

The notion of modernization was the most significant difference between the French and American approaches to counterrevolutionary warfare. Proponents of this idea, which emerged in American universities around the middle of the twentieth century but had roots deep in the American experience, as well as in what came to be known as New Deal liberalism, held that there was a fundamental difference between traditional and modern societies (Latham; Ekbladh). In the former, customary and religious ideas, practices, and authorities ruled human life, directing the lives of individuals and shaping the social, economic, and political worlds in which they passed their lives. In the latter, authority rested with individuals whose decisions directed politics, drove economies, and shaped social interaction. In a traditional society, the elders ruled. In a modern society, officials governed through bureaucracies but only at the pleasure of the electorate. In a traditional society, religious law or custom might determine when and where a market could take place, what could be sold, and who could sell it. In a modern society, individuals were free to buy and sell where and when and what they liked. In a traditional society, parents determined whom their children married, guided by notions of caste or class. In a modern society, children made marriage choices for themselves based on personal attachment. The transition from traditional to modern society, driven by technological development and economic growth, was disturbing, as all revolutions were, so it met with resistance and caused conflict. The communists, "scavengers of the modernization process" (Rostow 1961, 234), tried to exploit this conflict to lead modernizing societies down a path toward tyranny and poverty. The United States under the Kennedy administration was willing to wage counterinsurgency warfare, to struggle for the hearts and minds of the people in the new nations, to lead them onto the path toward freedom, democracy, and prosperity. The United States was doing this because it sought "to maintain an environment on the world scene which will permit our open society to survive and flourish" (236).

Despite the difference between the U.S. and French approaches, the U.S. effort to implement counterinsurgency, even most recently in Iraq and Afghanistan, has suffered from many of the same problems that affected the French. Both Mao and the Kennedy administration agreed that revolutionary warfare was a new and powerful kind of warfare. The U.S. military disagreed with both. It remained focused on nuclear conflict and a possible conventional war in Europe. It did so again when the Reagan administration sought to revive counterinsurgency in the 1980s. Even without the preoccupations of the Soviets and nuclear war, it was difficult after 9/11 to get the U.S. military geared up for counterinsurgency. In part, the blame for this rested with officials in the George W. Bush administration, who at first denied an insurgency was occurring in Iraq and then initially sought to end it by killing insurgents. Disputes as to how effective this latter strategy was continue, but at a minimum it would not have succeeded, as NSAM 182 predicted, without the Iraqis or Afghans taking up both the fight and sorting themselves out politically. The U.S. military, however, if less reluctant after 9/11 than in the past to take counterinsurgency seriously, proved, with some exceptions, not particularly competent at it (Tucker 2006, esp. 45–55; Lamb et al.; Flynn et al.) This should have been no more surprising than to discover that a heavy equipment operator was not adept at cabinetmaking.

The problems with American counterinsurgency efforts went well beyond a stroppy military. Throughout America's counterinsurgency labors, efforts to direct modernization or to assist new nations in taking the right path ran into the opposition of local elites, whose privileges and wealth were threatened by the kind of reforms and attention to grievances that theory and doctrine required. NSAM 182 recognized this problem but offered no solution, tending instead to assume that local elites would need only some encouragement to do the right thing (NSAM 182, 5, 11–12). Experiences subsequent to the drafting of the memorandum have not revealed a solution either. Neither did the United States develop particularly effective ways to coordinate its counterinsurgency efforts. Modernization was a social, economic, political, and psychological phenomenon, so the response to its problems had to be as well. This required the efforts of several different U.S. government organizations. The unity of this effort was to come in-country from the ambassador's leadership of the so-called country team, consisting of the heads of all the U.S. government organizations there. Yet even if an ambassador could manage to direct and unify the efforts of personnel from other agencies working out of his embassy (he did not control their budgets and did not determine their promotions so had little leverage over them), there was no effective mechanism to promote unity of effort in Washington (*Forging*). If the U.S. military deployed in large numbers to a country, as it did in Vietnam, Iraq, and Afghanistan, it was almost entirely outside the authority of the ambassador, as far as the details of its operations were concerned. Various U.S. government agencies could and did work at cross-purposes.

Beyond these difficulties with counterinsurgency doctrine and policy lay the problems of modernization theory itself (Tucker 1993, 36–38). The persistent assumption in American history has been that the course of western empire, and indeed human history, led toward one end-state: the United States, the first modern nation (Adams). The United States is "on the right side of history" (an idea used by both Condoleezza Rice, eventually George W. Bush's secretary of state, and, more frequently, by President Barack Obama [Rice; Pagoda]). If one assumed this to be the case, it made sense to assume that local elites, the civil servants and others Rostow spoke of, would sooner or later end up where American officials were, that it would be easier than it turned out to be to usher them and their countries into the modern world. Democracy would bloom, once the weeds that choked it, like Saddam Hussein, were removed. This view tended to discount what the locals thought and preferred. After all, they were traditionalists thinking in traditional and, so the modernists thought, soon to be obsolete ways. Rostow insisted that America was not imposing its system on the new nations. They were free to choose. Yet he was confident that they would choose liberal democracy (Rostow 1961, 235). As he indicated, the United States had a strong interest in the choice of democracy (NSAM 182, 10). This interest, combined with the presumed sanction of historical inevitability, meant in practice that the new nations were free to choose their political system, as long as they chose liberal democracy. Finally, since the inevitable movement of history was figured in the steady development of technology and the evidence of economic growth or "take off," as Rostow referred to it, a tendency existed to focus on the supposed economic causes of insurgency, even though Rostow argued that this was too narrow a view (Rostow 1960, 2, 121). Rostow was right. The causes of conflict cannot be reduced to deprivation or economic grievance, and grievances themselves are not sufficient to bring about conflict, let alone revolution (Tucker 2012, 50–75). In these different ways, modernization theory and the even more widely held assumption that the United States is the end point of human history led to misdiagnoses of the causes of unrest and how to treat it.

If the United States is not the end toward which history inevitably marches, then making the world like the United States will require more coercion, applied for a longer time, than modernization or democratization proponents suppose. Indeed, humans seem to hold tenaciously to their traditional ways of doing things. This explains why coercion played such a role in the history of imperialism. There was a reason why the old-fashioned imperialists relied on the exemplary atrocity and the bribe. The anti-imperialists and revolutionaries learned this lesson as well. Resentment of Euro-American empire created fertile ground for revolutionary mobilizers, but the revolutionaries, when they challenged traditional attachments, found it necessary to use coercion as often as the imperialists had. Similarly, just as the fancied heaven on earth the revolution would supposedly bring about justified the cruelty of its birthing, modernization theory was imperialism with a good conscience. Americans, like humanitarians, could remake the world in their image, assured that in doing so they were not imposing their will on others, merely helping history impose its purpose on them. This, of course, was a secular view of the nineteenth-century Christian justification of empire, the logic of history replacing the will of God.

Mention of the will of God brings us to the newest manifestation of anti-imperialism, the Islamist attack on America. In the last chapter I discussed the role of violence in this anti-imperial effort, arguing that it was similar to the claims for violence made by Begin and Fanon. The Islamist resistance, at least according to one of its leaders, was similar to older resistance movements in other ways as well. In explaining to Abu Musab al-Zarqawi, the leader of al-Qaeda in Iraq, why circulating videotapes of beheadings might not benefit the resistance, Ayman al-Zawahiri, now the head of al-Qaeda, walked Zarqawi through the resistance strategy we have encountered repeatedly. Given the disparities in power between America and the Faithful, if Islamic rule—the caliphate—is to come about, he wrote, it will come about only through jihad; jihad in turn will succeed only with popular support, gained by exploiting popular discontent. Only with popular support can the jihad movement avoid being crushed by the power of its enemies. Mobilizing popular support requires political fieldwork, which can best be done by coordinating political and military or violent action. "More than half this battle," Zawahiri wrote, "is a media battle, . . . a race for the hearts and minds of the" Muslim community (Zawahiri, 2, 3, 4, 5).

Zawahiri was encouraging Zarqawi to adopt a strategy that other Muslims have found effective. In the early twentieth century, the Muslim Brotherhood established itself in Egypt by providing social services that the government did not, then developing a clandestine military wing. Mobilizing the people through the subversive operation of an alternative government has allowed the Brotherhood to resist bouts of repression. Hezbollah in Lebanon and Hamas in the West Bank and Gaza followed the same strategy. In Afghanistan, reportedly, people use the Taliban's courts to settle property disputes and other matters because these courts are speedier and less corrupt than the government's. Islamic State, the successor organization to Zarqawi's, also provides governance and mixes efforts to win hearts and minds with its brutality as a way to mobilize support (Weiss and Hassan, 224–28). Thus, at the beginning of the twenty-first century, writing perhaps not far from where Dening had fought a hundred years before, Zawahiri summarized the lessons that anti-imperialists had learned by Dening's time and continued to perfect.

Reviewing the development of anti-imperialism makes clear that imperial policing became counterinsurgency after guerrilla warfare became insurgency. These were not mere changes in terminology but signified a change in conflict caused by a revolution in morality and an innovation in warfare. Imperialism rested on coercion; the European moral revolution limited the use of coercion. The anti-imperialists lacked coercive power; popular mobilization increased their coercive power. As the imperialists' ability to apply force decreased, the ability of the anti-imperialists to apply force increased. Counterinsurgency was a response to this development. It was meant to replace imperial policing—or rather, it was imperial policing within the limits of the moral revolution and adapted to the new coercive measures of the anti-imperialists. The traditional way to defeat resistance to imperial sway was to pursue the dispersed enemy relentlessly with mobile columns and destroy what could not disperse: crops, settlements, and often noncombatants. Search and destroy in Vietnam was the same tactic, in theory without the destruction of settlements and civilians. Practice did not always coincide with theory, however, and counterinsurgency proved less effective than hoped.

Conclusion

Euro-American imperialists and those who resisted them have been locked in a slowly evolving violent interaction for several hundred years. Unable to resist the overwhelming power of the imperialists in acute warfare, the anti-imperialists resorted to skulking as a version of chronic warfare. Unable to bring their skulking enemies to battle, the Euro-Americans responded with the mobile column and the exemplary atrocity. Warriors dispersing to skulk left vulnerable to imperialist violence what could not disperse or move quickly (their families, homes, and fields), creating opportunities for such atrocities. With these military means, the transforming and invigorating power of commerce and religion, and superior ability to extract resources from what they controlled, imperialists were able to contrive enduring, if contested, rule. As they enjoyed this rule, its ground slowly eroded. Doubts about the morality of empire gained currency. Religion became more and more a humanitarian sentiment, and a growing concern for human rights validated colonial resistance.

At roughly the same time, the anti-imperialists learned to use nationalism and revolutionary reeducation and social restructuring to increase their ability to extract resources from colonial populations. They combined popular mobilization with skulking or guerrilla warfare and terrorism (targeting civilians) to produce insurgency. Anti-imperialists also learned to play on doubts about empire, applying the imperialists' language of rights to themselves, even quoting the Declaration of Independence. In these ways, the anti-imperialists learned to counter what had been the overwhelming physical and moral advantages of the imperialists. The imperialists responded with what became known as counterinsurgency, which was imperial polic-

ing within the new moral limits. The more difficult task of addressing grievances replaced the exemplary atrocity, at least in principle.

Commerce played a key role in imperialism. When they first began their
imperial activities, the European powers followed the principles of mercantilism, the view that controlling trade, rather than freeing it, was the way to
wealth. This was part of the reason that the European powers sought political control over foreign territory, what we customarily recognize as empire.
Political control allowed unfettered extraction of resources (gold, silver, fur)
and monopoly control of the economic activity of the seized territory. Eventually Europeans, especially the British, came to value free trade and sought
to impose it as a practice, even as they kept direct political control. The
United States joined in this activity, using coercion at first as the Europeans
did. After World War II, through its dominance of the world economy and
the international organizations that regulate it, the United States pressed
for economic liberalization, even as Europeans became more skeptical of it.

The regime of economic liberalism differs from mercantile empire in various ways, but the most important is that free trade rests on the idea that
both parties benefit from the trade. Mutual benefit means that coercion is
not necessary. Mercantilism assumed that only one side benefited in a trade.
No one gained unless someone lost. Contemporary opponents of free trade,
those who oppose the so-called neocolonialism of liberalism, do not believe
in its mutual benefit. Thus, they are more inclined to be coercive or, the
same thing, supportive of governments that regulate or directly control economic activity. Of course, in making everyone richer, free trade may make
some richer than others. It would be unjust, however, to object to alleviating
the poverty of many because of the greater wealth of a few. This is especially
so since the illiberal alternative, without making everyone richer, still makes
some richer than others. In any event, the transition to free trade, or at least
away from strict mercantilism, meant that much of the economic or commercial reason for imperialism disappeared (access to resources remained a
concern) at about the same time that its moral rationale did. The emergence
of insurgency as an anti-imperialist strategy, then, made maintaining imperial control more costly as the value of imperialism, as political control over
space through time, declined.

On balance, it seems reasonable to conclude that imperialism declined
primarily because of changes to the moral and economic reasoning of the
imperialists and their domestic populations rather than because of the

effectiveness of insurgency and terrorism as anti-imperial strategies. Certainly, the European powers were weak after World War II, but the United States was willing to support their efforts against communists in the remnants of their empires, if not to sustain their imperial designs. Many proponents of insurgency (Mao Zedong, for example) would accept the judgment that imperial defeat was political and economic, rather than military. Insurgency and terrorism were for them a necessary step on the path of mobilizing resources for a conventional military-political struggle. They were not intended to be sufficient as an anti-imperialist strategy. By and large, they were not (Tucker 2014, 195–97). It is, of course, possible to pick out one case in which the imperialist was both unusually weak and inept and show that terrorism and insurgency worked (Hoffman). But in this case—the struggle for Palestine—the moral balance of forces heavily favored the Jews over the British, reinforcing the conclusion that this balance was critical to the outcome of the struggle between imperial and anti-imperialist power.

Assessing the relative importance of the factors in the imperial collapse is complicated by several things, principally perhaps the fact that during the twentieth century, when that collapse occurred, the Euro-American powers were preoccupied with internal Euro-American conflicts. This meant that they could not focus their considerable resources on the imperial issue, even if they had been willing to. It also meant that their armies focused on acute rather than chronic warfare and often, therefore, not surprisingly, proved themselves inept at the latter. In truth, this result occurred not just for geopolitical reasons but because of the military traditions that have evolved in modern nation-states over hundreds of years. During the period between the collapse of the Soviet Union and the wars in Afghanistan and Iraq, the U.S. military was primarily involved in chronic warfare, yet it was unprepared for such warfare in either of those countries. The political leadership that sent the military into those wars did not help it adapt to the kind of war it found there, but those leaders cannot bear all of the blame for the failures that ensued.

Euro-American militaries are likely to have further opportunities to test their ability to adapt to chronic warfare. The economic form in which Euro-American power now most affects the world seems likely to promote continued resistance, because economic liberalization affects more than trade. It affects domestic economic activity and politics, even family life and the ways individuals live. It touches the heart of human existence and alters its rhythm. For this reason, like other aspects of modernization, it has created resistance. Individual initiative is at the heart of economic and political liberalism because it is the heart of freedom, but such initiative threatens custom, established power, and time-honored privilege. Since at least the Amerindians of North America at the time of Pontiac's rebellion, many affected by liberalization or modernization or globalization have organized to resist it. They have asserted the superiority of ancestral ways and even used violence and the latest technology to defend those ways. This nostalgic longing for an imagined past, mixed with modernism (i.e., the use of technology that did not exist in that imagined past), was a strand in the fabric of fascism (cf. Paxton, 12–13). This is one way to understand the violent Islamic resistance movement that developed in the twentieth century and attacked the United States on September 11, 2001. It is not essentially different from the Amerindian attack on Detroit and other settlements in 1763.

As with previous modern efforts to defend ancestral ways, the Islamist version is as much modern as ancient, innovative as customary, if not more so (Gesnik). Its modernity is evident not principally in its strategy, tactics, or technology but in the fact that Islamism, like National Socialism and Marxism-Leninism, claims that there is a final solution available in this world to the problems that plague human beings. The rule of the devout, the master race, or the master class will fix everything. This is what the Islamists mean when they say "Islam is the answer." A spokesman for the so-called Islamic State, the successor organization to the one that Zarqawi started, said "we aim to build an Islamic state to cover every aspect of life" (Packer). Religions that emphasize the transcendence of God typically acknowledge as a consequence that only God is purely good and that no human institution, including religious institutions, can be purely good. This understanding tempers claims for justice, for making a heaven on earth, for having all the answers, for solving all of mankind's problems. In saying that they seek to build an Islamic state to cover every aspect of life, Islamists are saying, in effect, that they will leave nothing to chance or, as the truly pious would say, leave nothing to God. Islamism is a kind of atheism, therefore. It believes that human efforts, human hands, technology of one sort or another, can build a heaven on earth. It thus shows itself to be, like National Socialism and Marxism-Leninism, a radicalized version of the modern reliance on human initiative that led to the imperialism the Islamists so hate. Liberal democracies also derive from this modern emphasis on individual initiative, but they show their moderation, and their piety, by separating church and state. This is a tacit admission that in this world, there is no final solution. Justice is in the hands of God. (For a Christian acknowledgement of this dilemma, see Mark 10:18 and Luke 18:19, and context).

Similar to Marxism-Leninism in tactics, strategy, objective, and core beliefs (Hansen and Kainz; Tucker 2012, 202–4), Islamism is likely to continue to present an insurgent threat. How will the post-imperial Euro-Americans meet it? Their power and their ability to project it over space through time far surpasses that of their enemies. Drone strikes in remote areas of Afghanistan are a frequent reminder of this. Applying military and other forms of power creates problems, however. Western influence or control or even presence gives energy to Islamism. Euro-Americans, therefore, should meet the threat through local authorities who are also threatened. Past experience suggests the limitations of this approach, however. Local authorities may be inept or corrupt and will undoubtedly have interests that conflict with those of the Euro-Americans who try to work with them. These problems will persist and hamper effective response.

The problems posed by local authorities, as well as geopolitical realities, will undoubtedly mean that dealing with Islamism will require dealing with the regional powers that have emerged or will emerge in the post-imperial world. China, Russia, and Iran all have problems with Islamism. That might suggest the possibility of alliances of convenience in some places at some times to deal with the threat. Such an approach—taking into account China's Muslim problem, for example, deemphasizing America's unique interests, and building coalitions—might defuse Great Power conflict while dealing effectively with the threat of radicalized Islam. This approach would also encourage efforts against the proliferation of weapons technology, particularly weapons derived from man's increasing power over human biology. This technological threat is what ultimately may make Islamism most dangerous. Interests among the various powers are so different and so strong, however, that one cannot be optimistic that this multilateral approach will be possible. The Euro-Americans, then, are most likely to find themselves needing to deal effectively with both emerging regional powers and various regional insurgencies. In both cases, some of their antagonists will be both willing and able to project their power into the Euro-American homeland, a continuing reversal of the pattern of the last several hundred years. In this case, the Euro-Americans would have to find some way to balance their efforts so that they can deal both with insurgency and a great power conflict at the same time. Neither the United States nor any European power managed to do this during the Cold War (Tucker 2006, esp. 64–68).

Beyond the issues of geopolitical and strategic calculation lie the political and moral issues of especial importance in understanding the rise and fall of Euro-American empire. The problem here is not principally the enervating or paralyzing effects of post-imperial guilt. Some expression of this guilt occurred in the aftermath of the 9/11 attacks but had little or no political effect. In fact, if it had any, it served more to rally American morale than to undermine it. In this post-imperial age, the issue for the former imperialists is not imposing their will on others but surviving the attempted imposition of the others' will. Unlike conquest, self-defense presents no moral problems, returning the moral advantage to the imperialists or at least removing the moral disadvantage they labored under, at least in their own eyes. This should make the use of force to combat Islamists easier than its use was to maintain empire. Certainly, after the cost of efforts in Iraq and Afghanistan, Euro-Americans are now reluctant to address Islamism overseas. For the long term, if the threat persists, as continuing attacks in the Euro-American homeland suggest it will, the evidence from America's post-Vietnam experience indicates the reluctance will fade. The moral restraint Americans impose on their government is malleable and decreases as the perceived threat increases (Lyte; Zegart; Gronke and Rejali).

The future and consequences of the more fundamental moral problem are incalculable. The great European going-out-over-the-world relied on convictions that weakened as empire grew. Technological power increased as moral certainty declined. Man-made technological power can now destroy the world, yet man-made norms cannot give it meaning. Post-imperial guilt is an epiphenomenon of the gradual hollowing out of Euro-American self-confidence. Reflecting on this hollowing, a man thought by some to be the greatest thinker of the twentieth century insisted "only a god can still save us" (Heidegger, 277). The Islamists think they have that saving God. The future, then, may be a contest between their solid conviction and the mere Euro-American desire for self-preservation, suggesting perhaps a worryingly unequal moral contest. But one may still hope that the confrontation with Islamists and other enemies will become one of the fundamental experiences from which Americans recover and strengthen conviction about the inherent goodness of their own way of life. As Shakespeare has King Henry say of the courage that the English should derive, the night before the battle of Agincourt, from confronting the French threat, "God almighty,/There is some soul of goodness in things evil,/Would men observingly distill it out" (Shakespeare, IV.1.4–5).

Facing this future, we might recall words spoken in the midst of the Cold War. Walt Rostow, one of the war's architects, explained its purpose as a defense of America's ancestral ways, "the old humane lines which go back to our birth as a nation—and which reach deeper into history than that—back to the Mediterranean roots of Western life" (Rostow 1961, 235–36). We see now that when Rostow spoke of the Mediterranean roots of Western life, he was referring to the common root of Judaism, Christianity, and Islam, as well as to the different root represented by Athens and Rome. The separation of church and state is the modern expression of how these separate roots combine in modern Western life. That is still a way of life worth defending.

References

Abernethy, David B. *The Dynamics of Global Dominance: European Overseas Empires, 1415–1980*. New Haven: Yale University Press, 2002.

Abun-Nasr, Jamil M. *Muslim Communities of Grace: The Sufi Brotherhoods in Islamic Religious Life*. New York: Columbia University Press, 2007.

Adams, John Quincy. *An Address, Delivered at the Request of the Committee of Arrangements for Celebrating the Declaration of Independence, at the City of Washington on the Fourth of July 1821, upon the Occasion of Reading the Declaration of Independence*. Cambridge: Printed at the University Press by Hilliard & Metcalf, 1821.

Allard, Gen. Jacques. "Verités sur l'affaire algerienne." *Revue de Défense Nationale* 26 (January 1958): 5–41.

Ambler, John Stewart. *The French Army in Politics, 1954–1962*. Columbus: Ohio State University Press, 1966.

Ammon, Harry. *James Monroe: The Quest for National Identity*. Charlottesville: University Press of Virginia, 1990.

Anderson, Fred. *Crucible of War: The Seven Years' War and the Fate of Empire in British North America, 1754–1766*. New York: Vintage, 2000.

Arreguin-Toft, M. Ivan. *How the Weak Win Wars: A Theory of Asymmetric Conflict*. Cambridge: Cambridge University Press, 2005.

Bakewell, Peter. "Conquest after the Conquest: The Rise of Spanish Domination in America." In *Spain, Europe, and the Atlantic World: Essays in Honor of John H. Elliott*, ed. Richard L. Kagan and Geoffrey Parker. Cambridge: Cambridge University Press, 1995.

Barnett, Michael. *Empire of Humanity: A History of Humanitarianism*. Ithaca, NY: Cornell University Press, 2013.

Bayly, C. E. *Empire and Information: Intelligence Gathering and Social Communication in India, 1780–1870*. Cambridge: Cambridge University Press, 2000.

Beckett, Ian F. W. *Modern Insurgencies and Counter-Insurgencies: Guerrillas and Their Opponents since 1750*. New York: Routledge, 2001.

Begin, Menachem. *The Revolt: The Story of the Irgun*. Jerusalem: Steimatzky, 1977.

Bender, Thomas. *The Antislavery Debate: Capitalism and Abolitionism as a Problem in Historical Interpretation*. Berkeley: University of California Press, 1992.

Berinsky, Adam J. *In Time of War: Understanding American Public Opinion from World War II to Iraq*. Chicago: University of Chicago Press, 2009.

Biddle, Stephen. "Allies, Airpower, and Modern Warfare: The Afghan Model in Afghanistan and Iraq." *International Security* 30, no. 3 (Winter 2005–6): 161–76.

———. *Military Power: Explaining Victory and Defeat in Modern Battle*. Princeton: Princeton University Press, 2004.

Black, Jeremy. "The Military Revolution II: The Eighteenth-Century." In *The Oxford History of Modern War*, ed. Charles Townshend. New York: Oxford University Press, 2005.

——. *Warfare in the Western World, 1882–1975*. Bloomington: Indiana University Press, 2002.

Bourgès-Maunoury, Maurice. "Le Problème algerien." *Revue Militaire d'Information* 274 (July 1956): 6–7.

Brady, Thomas A. "The Rise of Merchant Empires, 1400–1700: A European Counterpoint." In *The Political Economy of Merchant Empires: State Power and World Trade, 1350–1750*, ed. James D. Tracy. Cambridge: Cambridge University Press, 1997.

Brewer, John. "The Eighteenth-Century British State: Contexts and Issues." In *An Imperial State at War: Britain from 1869–1815*, ed. Lawrence Stone. New York: Routledge, 1993.

——. *The Sinews of Power: War, Money, and the English State, 1688–1783*. Cambridge, MA: Harvard University Press, 1988.

Bryant, G. J. "Asymmetric Warfare: The British Experience in Eighteenth-Century India." *Journal of Military History* 68, no. 2 (April 2004): 431–69.

Calloway, Colin G. *New Worlds for All: Indians, Europeans, and the Remaking of Early America*. Baltimore: Johns Hopkins University Press, 2013.

Callwell, C. E. *Small Wars: Their Principles and Practice*. 1896. Reprint, Lincoln: University of Nebraska Press, 1996.

Childs, John. "The Military Revolution I: The Transition to Modern Warfare." In *The Oxford History of Modern War*, ed. Charles Townshend. New York: Oxford University Press, 2005.

Chinh, Truong. *Selected Writings*. Moscow: Foreign Language Publishing House, 1977.

Colby, Elbridge. "How to Fight Savage Tribes." *American Journal of International Law* 21, no. 2 (April 1927): 279–88.

Crane, R. S. "Suggestions toward a Genealogy of the Man of Feeling." *ELH: English Literary History* 1, no. 3 (December 1934): 205–30.

Davis, David Brion. *Inhuman Bondage: The Rise and Fall of Slavery in the New World*. New York: Oxford University Press, 2006.

Dening, Maj. B. C. "Modern Problems of Guerilla Warfare." *Army Quarterly and Defence Journal* 13 (1926): 347–54.

Diamond, Jared. *Guns, Germs, and Steel: The Fates of Human Societies*. New York: W. W. Norton, 1998.

Dowd, Gregory Evans. *War under Heaven: Pontiac, the Indian Nations, and the British Empire*. Baltimore: Johns Hopkins University Press, 2002.

Duffy, Michael. "World-Wide War and British Expansion, 1793–1815." In *The Oxford History of the British Empire, Volume II: The Eighteenth Century*, ed. P. J. Marshall. New York: Oxford University Press, 1998.

Ekbladh, David. *The American Mission: Modernization and the Construction of an American World Order*. Princeton: Princeton University Press, 2010.

Elliott, J. H. "The Spanish Conquest." In *Colonial Spanish America*, ed. Leslie Bethell. Cambridge: Cambridge University Press, 1987.

English, Richard. *Armed Struggle: The History of the IRA*. London: Pan Books, 2012.

Entman, Robert W. *Projections of Power: Framing News, Public Opinion, and U.S. Foreign Policy*. Chicago: University of Chicago Press, 2003.

Evans, Gareth. "The Responsibility to Protect: Rethinking Humanitarian Intervention." *Proceedings of the American Society of International Law* 98 (2004): 78–89.

Evans, Martin. *Algeria: France's Undeclared War*. New York: Oxford University Press, 2012.

Fall, Bernard B. *Street Without Joy: The French Debacle in Indochina*. New York: Schocken, 1972.

Fanon, Frantz. *The Wretched of the Earth*, trans. Constance Farrington, preface by Jean-Paul Sartre. New York: Grove, 1966.

Feaver, Peter. *Armed Servants: Agency, Oversight, and Civil-Military Relations*. Cambridge, MA: Harvard University Press, 2005.

Fiering, Norman S. "Irresistible Compassion: An Aspect of Eighteenth-Century Sympathy and Humanitarianism." *Journal of the History of Ideas* 3, no. 2 (April–June, 1976): 195–218.

Findlay, Ronald, and Kevin O'Rourke. *Power and Plenty: Trade, War, and the World Economy in the Second Millennium*. Princeton: Princeton University Press, 2009.

Firestone, Reuven. "Conception of Holy War in Biblical and Qur'anic Tradition." *Journal of Religious Ethics* 24, 1 (Spring 1996): 99–123.

Flynn, Maj. Gen. Michael T., USA, Capt. Matt Pottinger, USMC, and Paul D. Batchelor. *Fixing Intel: A Blueprint for Making Intelligence Relevant in Afghanistan*. Washington, DC: Center for a New American Security, January 2010.

Franklin, Benjamin. *Benjamin Franklin's Autobiography*. New York: W. W. Norton, 1986.

French, David. *The British Way in Counterinsurgency, 1945–1967*. Oxford: Oxford University Press, 2011.

Friedberg, Aaron. *In the Shadow of the Garrison State: America's Anti-Statism and Its Cold War Strategy*. Princeton: Princeton University Press, 2000.

Fukuyama, Francis. *The Origins of Political Order: From Prehuman Times to the French Revolution*. New York: Farrar, Straus and Giroux, 2011.

Géré, François. *La Guerre psychologique*. Paris: Economica, 1997.

Gesnik, Indira Falk. "'Chaos on Earth': Subjective Truths versus Communal Unity in Islamic Law and the Rise of Militant Islam." *American Historical Review* 103 (2003): 710–33.

Grenier, John. *The First Way of War: American War Making on the Frontier, 1607–1814*. Cambridge: Cambridge University Press, 2008.

Gronke, Paul, and Darius Rejali, with Dustin Drenguis, James Hicks, Peter Miller, and Bryan Nakayama. "U.S. Public Opinion on Torture, 2001–2009." *PS: Political Science and Politics*, July 2010, 437–44.

Hansen, Hendrik, and Peter Kainz. "Radical Islamism and Totalitarian Ideology: A Comparison of Sayyid Qutb's Islamism with Marxism and National Socialism." *Totalitarian Movements and Political Religions* 8, no. 1 (March 2007): 55–76.

Headrick, Daniel R. *Power over Peoples: Technology, Environments, and Western Imperialism, 1400 to the Present*. Princeton: Princeton University Press, 2009.

Heidegger, Martin. "Only a God Can Save Us: *Der Spiegel*'s Interview with Martin Heidegger." *Philosophy Today* 20 (Winter 1976): 267–84.

Hemming, John. *The Conquest of the Incas*. New York: Harcourt Brace Jovanovich, 1970.

Hoffman, Bruce. *Anonymous Soldiers: The Struggle for Israel, 1917–1947*. New York: Alfred A. Knopf, 2015.

Horne, Alistair. *A Savage War of Peace: Algeria 1954–1962*. London: Macmillan, 1977.

Jefferson, Thomas. *Thomas Jefferson: Writings*, ed. Merrill D. Peterson. New York: Library of America, 1984.

"John Bowyer Bell." Obituary. *Telegraph*, October 15, 2003.

Jones, Timothy Llewellyn. "The Development of British Counterinsurgency Policies and Doctrine, 1945–52." Ph.D. diss., University of London, 1991.

Keddie, Nikki R. "The Revolt of Islam, 1700 to 1993: Comparative Considerations and Relations to Imperialism." *Comparative Studies in Society and History* 36, no. 3 (July 1993): 463–87.

Keegan, John. *The Face of Battle: A Study of Agincourt, Waterloo, and the Somme*. New York: Viking Press, 1976.

Kennedy, John F. "Remarks at West Point to the Graduating Class of the U.S. Military Academy, June 6, 1962." *The Public Papers of the Presidents, John F. Kennedy, 1962*. Washington, DC: Government Printing Office, 1977.

Kiernan, V. G. *Colonial Empires and Armies: 1815–1960*. Guernsey, Channel Islands: Sutton Publishing Limited, 1998.

Kingdon, John W. *Agendas, Alternatives, and Public Policies*, 2nd ed. New York: Longman, 2002.

Krepinevich, Andrew. "Cavalry to Computer: The Pattern of Military Revolutions." *National Interest* 37 (Fall 1994): 30–42.

Lacheroy, Col. Charles. *La Guerre revolutionnaire*. Paris: Presses Universitaires de France, 1958.

Lamb, Christopher Jon, Matthew Schmidt, and Berit Fitzsimmons. "MRAPs, Irregular Warfare, and Pentagon Reform." Occasional Paper, Institute for National Strategic Studies, National Defense University, June 2009.

Landers, John. *The Field and the Forge: Population, Production, and Power in the Pre-industrial West*. New York: Oxford University Press, 2003.

Larkin, Maurice. *France since the Popular Front: Government and People, 1936–1996*, 2nd ed. Oxford: Clarendon Press, 1997.

Larson, Eric V., and Bogdan Savych. *American Public Support for U.S. Military Operations from Mogadishu to Baghdad*. Santa Monica, CA: RAND, 2005.

———. *Misfortunes of War: Press and Public Reactions to Civilian Deaths in Wartime*. Santa Monica, CA: RAND, 2006.

Larson, Mark. "The Holy War Trajectory among the Reformed: From Zurich to England." *Reformation and Renaissance Review* 8, no. 1 (February 2006): 7–27.

Latham, Michael E. *The Right Kind of Revolution: Modernization, Development, and U.S. Foreign Policy from the Cold War to the Present*. Ithaca, NY: Cornell University Press, 2011.

Ledwidge, Frank. *Losing Small Wars: British Military Failure in Iraq and Afghanistan*. New Haven: Yale University Press, 2011.

Lee, Wayne E. *Barbarians and Brothers: Anglo-American Warfare, 1500–1865*. New York: Oxford University Press, 2011.

Leites, Nathan, and Charles Wolfe Jr. *Rebellion and Authority: An Analytic Essay on Insurgent Conflicts*. Santa Monica, CA: RAND, 1970.

Logevall, Frederik. *Embers of War: The Fall of an Empire and the Making of America's Vietnam*. New York: Random House, 2013.

Lyte, Brittany. "Americans Have Grown More Supportive of Torture," *FiveThirtyEight*, December 9, 2014, http://fivethirtyeight.com/datalab/senate-torture-report-public-opinion/.

MacCulloch, Diarmaid. *The Reformation: A History*. New York: Penguin Books, 2003.

MacMaster, Neil. "The Roots of Insurrection: The Role of the Algerian Village Assembly

(Djemâa) in Peasant Resistance, 1863–1962." *Comparative Studies in Society and History* 55, no. 2 (April 2013): 419–47.

Mao Tse-Tung. *On Guerrilla Warfare*, trans. and with an introduction by Samuel B. Griffith. New York: Praeger, 1961.

———. *Selected Works*, Volume 2. Beijing: Foreign Language Press, 1967.

Marshall, P. J. "The British in Asia: Trade to Dominion, 1700–1765." In *The Oxford History of the British Empire, Volume II: The Eighteenth Century*, ed. P. J. Marshall. New York: Oxford University Press, 1998.

McMahon, Deidre. "Ireland and the Empire-Commonwealth, 1900–1948." In *The Oxford History of the British Empire, Volume IV: The Twentieth Century*, ed. Judith Brown and Wm. Roger Louis. New York: Oxford University Press, 1999.

Merom, Gil. *How Democracies Lose Small Wars: State, Society, and the Failures of France in Algeria, Israel in Lebanon, and the United States in Vietnam*. Cambridge: Cambridge University Press, 2003.

Ministère de la Défense nationale et des Force Armées, État Major Defense Armées, 5e division. *Instruction provisoire sur l'emploi de l'arme psychologique*. Paris: Ministère de la Défense nationale et des Force Armées, État Major Defense Armées, 5e division, July 29, 1957.

Mitrovich, Gregory. *Undermining the Kremlin: America's Strategy to Subvert the Soviet Bloc, 1947–1956*. Ithaca, NY: Cornell University Press, 2000.

Moreman, T. R. "'Small Wars' and 'Imperial Policing': The British Army and the Theory and Practice of Colonial Warfare in the British Empire, 1919–1939." *Journal of Strategic Studies* 19, no. 4 (December 1996): 105–31.

Morris, Ian. *Why the West Rules—for Now: The Patterns of History, and What They Reveal about the Future*. New York: Farrar, Straus and Giroux, 2010.

Motadel, David. Introduction to *Islam and the European Empires*, ed. David Motadel. New York: Oxford University Press, 2014.

———. "Islam and the European Empires." *Historical Journal* 55, no. 3 (2012): 831–56.

National Security Council. "United States Overseas Internal Defense Policy." National Security Action Memorandum 182, August 24, 1962. Reprinted in *Foreign Relations of the United States, 1961–1963, Volumes VII/VIII/IX, Microfiche Supplement, Arms Control; National Security; Foreign Economic Policy*, Document 279, https://history.state.gov/historicaldocuments/frus1961-63v07-09mSupp/d279. Washington, DC: Government Printing Office, 1997.

Overy, Richard. "The Second World War: A Barbarous Conflict?" In *The Barbarization of Warfare*, ed. George Kassimeris. New York: New York University Press, 2006.

Packer, George. "The Common Enemy." *New Yorker*, August 25, 2014.

Pagden, Anthony. *Lords of All the World: Ideologies of Empire in Spain, Britain, and France, 1500–1800*. New Haven: Yale University Press, 1998.

Pape, Robert. *Bombing to Win: Air Power and Coercion in War*. Ithaca, NY: Cornell University Press, 1996.

Parker, Jeffrey. "Early Modern Europe." In *The Laws of War: Constraints on Warfare in the Western World*, ed. Michael Howard, George Andreopoulos, and Mark R. Shulman. New Haven: Yale University Press, 1997.

Parmelee, Maurice. "The Rise of Modern Humanitarianism." *American Journal of Sociology* 21, no. 3 (November 1915): 345–59.

Parry, J. H. *The Age of Reconnaissance: Discovery, Exploration, and Settlement, 1450 to 1650*. Berkeley: University of California Press, 1981.

————. *Establishment of the European Hegemony, 1415–1715: Trade and Exploration in the Age of the Renaissance*. New York: Harper and Row, 1961.

Paxton, Robert O. *The Anatomy of Fascism*. New York: Alfred A. Knopf, 2004.

Pearson, M. N. "Merchants and States." In *The Political Economy of Merchant Empires: State Power and World Trade, 1350–1750*, ed. James D. Tracy. Cambridge: Cambridge University Press, 1997.

Peters, Rudolph. *Islam and Colonialism: The Doctrine of Jihad in Modern History*. The Hague: Mouton, 1979.

Planchais, Jean. "Petite histoire de l'action psychologique." *Signes du Temps* 1 (January 1959): 11–14.

Porter, Andrew. "Religion, Missionary Enthusiasm, and Empire." In *The Oxford History of the British Empire, Volume III: The Nineteenth-Century*. New York: Oxford University Press, 1999.

Project on National Security Reform. *Forging a New Shield*. Washington, DC: Project on National Security Reform, 2008.

Ralston, David B. *Importing the European Army: The Introduction of European Military Techniques and Institutions in the Extra-European World, 1600–1914*. Chicago: University of Chicago Press, 1996.

Ray, Rajat Kanta. "Indian Society and the Establishment of British Supremacy, 1765–1818." In *The Oxford History of the British Empire, Volume II: The Eighteenth Century*, ed. P. J. Marshall. New York: Oxford University Press, 1998.

Rice, Condoleezza. "Campaign 2000: Promoting the National Interest." *Foreign Affairs*, February 7, 2015, www.foreignaffairs.com/articles/55630/condoleezza-rice/campaign-2000-promoting-the-national-interest.

Rioux, Jean-Pierre. *The Fourth Republic, 1944–1958*, trans. Godfrey Rogers. Cambridge: Cambridge University Press, 1987.

Roberts, Adam. "Land Warfare: From Hague to Nuremberg." In *The Laws of War: Constraints on Warfare in the Western World*, ed. Michael Howard, George Andreopoulos, and Mark R. Shulman. New Haven: Yale University Press, 1997.

Robinson, Francis. "The British Empire and the Muslim World." In *The Oxford History of the British Empire, Volume IV: The Twentieth Century*, ed. Judith Brown and Wm. Roger Louis. New York: Oxford University Press, 1999.

Rogers, Clifford J. *The Military Revolution Debate: Readings on the Military Transformation of Early Modern Europe*. Boulder: Westview Press, 1995.

Rostow, W. W. "Guerrilla Warfare in the Underdeveloped Areas." *Department of State Bulletin*, 45, no. 1154 (August 7, 1961).

————. *The Stages of Economic Growth: A Non-Communist Manifesto*, 3rd ed. Cambridge: Cambridge University Press, 1960.

Roy, Kaushik. "Military Synthesis in South Asia: Armies, Warfare, and Indian Society, c. 1740–1849." *Journal of Military History* 69, no. 3 (July 2005): 651–90.

Russell, Peter. "Redcoats in the Wilderness: British Officers and Irregular Warfare in Europe and America, 1740 to 1760." *William and Mary Quarterly* 35 (1978): 629–52.

Sayer, Derek. "British Reaction to the Amritsar Massacre, 1919–1920." *Past and Present* 131 (May 1991): 130–64.

Shafer, D. Michael. *Deadly Paradigms: The Failure of U.S. Counterinsurgency Policy*. Princeton: Princeton University Press, 1988.

Shakespeare, William. *The Life of Henry the Fifth*, ed. Barbara A. Mowat and Paul Werstine. New York: Simon and Schuster Paperbacks, 1995.

Skinner, Rob, and Alan Lester. "Humanitarianism and Empire: New Research Agendas." *Journal of Imperial and Commonwealth History* 40, 5 (December 2012): 729–47.

Stevenson, David. "Europe before 1914." www.bl.uk/world-war-one/articles/europe-before -1914.

Sullivan, Anthony Thrall. *Thomas-Robert Bugeaud: France and Algeria, 1784–1849*. Hamden, CT: Archon, 1983.

Summers, Harry G. *On Strategy: A Critical Analysis of the Vietnam War*. New York: Presidio, 1982.

Taşpınar, Ömer. "Fighting Radicalism, Not 'Terrorism': Root Causes of an International Actor Redefined." *SAIS Review* 29, no. 2 (Summer–Fall 2009): 75–86.

Taylor, Alan. *Colonial America: A Very Short Introduction*. Oxford: Oxford University Press, 2012.

Thomas, Keith. *Religion and the Decline of Magic*. New York: Scribner's, 1986.

Tilly, Charles. *Coercion, Capital and European States: AD 990–1992*. New York: Wiley-Blackwell, 1992.

Townshend, Charles. *Easter 1916: The Irish Rebellion*. Chicago: Ivan R. Dee, 2005.

Tripodi, Christian. "Peacemaking through Bribes or Cultural Empathy: The Political Officer and Britain's Strategy towards the North-West Frontier, 1901–1945." *Journal of Strategic Studies* 31 (February 2008): 123–51.

Tucker, David. *Confronting the Unconventional: Innovation and Transformation in Military Affairs*. Carlisle, PA: U.S. Army War College, 2006.

———. *The End of Intelligence: Espionage and State Power in the Information Age*. Stanford: Stanford University Press, 2014.

———. "Facing the Facts: The Failure of Nation Assistance." *Parameters* 23, 2 (Summer 1993): 34–40.

———. *Illuminating the Dark Arts of War: Terrorism, Sabotage, and Subversion in Homeland Security and the New Conflict*. New York: Continuum, 2012.

———. *Skirmishes at the Edge of Empire: The United States and International Terrorism*. Westport, CT: Praeger, 1997.

Tucker, David, and Christopher J. Lamb. *United States Special Operations Forces*. New York: Columbia University Press, 2007.

Vandervort, Bruce. *Wars of Imperial Conquest in Africa, 1830–1914*. Bloomington: Indiana University Press, 1998.

Vickery, Lt. Col. C. E. "Small Wars." *Army Quarterly* 6, no. 2 (July 1923): 307–17.

Vikør, Knut S. "Religious Revolts in Colonial North Africa." In *Islam and the European Empires*, ed. David Motadel. New York: Oxford University Press, 2014.

Viner, Jacob. "Power versus Plenty as Objectives of Foreign Policy in the Seventeenth and Eighteenth Centuries." *World Politics* 1, no. 1 (October 1948): 1–29.

Waldman, Carl. *Atlas of the North American Indian*, rev. ed. New York: Checkmark Books, 2000.

Weiss, Michael, and Hassan Hassan. *ISIS: Inside the Army of Terror*. New York: Regan Arts, 2015.

Woodberry, Robert. "The Missionary Roots of Liberal Democracy." *American Political Science Review* 106, no. 2 (May 2012): 244–74.

Yagoda, Ben. "Is Obama Overusing the Phrase *the Wrong Side of History*? Are We All?" *Slate*, April 17, 2014, www.slate.com/blogs/lexicon_valley/2014/04/17/the_phrase_the_wrong _side_of_history_around_for_more_than_a_century_is_getting.html.

Zawahiri, Ayman-al. "Letter to Zarqawi." Combating Terrorism Center at West Point, www .ctc.usma.edu/posts/zawahiris-letter-to-zarqawi-english-translation-2.

Zegart, Amy. "Controversy Dims as Public Opinion Shifts." *New York Times*, December 28, 2014, http://www.nytimes.com/roomfordebate/2013/01/07/the-right-or-wrong-expe rience-for-the-job/controversy-dims-as-public-opinion-shifts-5.

Zhai, Qiang. "Transplanting the Chinese Model: Chinese Military Advisers and the First Vietnam War, 1950–1954." *Journal of Military History* 57, no. 4 (1993): 689–715.

Index